Colin Wilson is one of the most prolific, versatile and popular writers at work today. He was born in Leicester in 1931, and left school at sixteen. After he had spent years working in a wool warehouse, a laboratory, a plastics factory and a coffee bar his first book *The Outsider* was published in 1956. It received outstanding critical acclaim and was an immediate bestseller.

Since then he has written many books on philosophy, the occult, crime and sexual deviance, plus a host of successful novels which have won him an international reputation. His work has been translated into Spanish, French, Swedish, Dutch, Japanese, German, Italian, Portuguese, Danish, Norwegian, Finnish and Hebrew.

By the same author

SUPER CONSCIOUSNESS

The Quest for the Peak Experience

Colin Wilson

WATKINS PUBLISHING

LONDON

Distributed in the USA and Canada by Sterling Publishing Co., Inc.
387 Park Avenue South, New York, NY 10016

This edition first published in the UK and USA 2009 by
Watkins Publishing, Sixth Floor, Castle House,
75–76 Wells Street, London W1T 3QH

1 3 5 7 9 10 8 6 4 2

Designed by Jerry Goldie

Printed and bound in Great Britain

Library of Congress Cataloging-in-Publication Data Available

ISBN: 978-1-906787-09-7

www.watkinspublishing.co.uk

For information about custom editions, special sales, premium and
corporate purchases, please contact Sterling Special Sales
Department at 800-805-5489 or specialsales@sterlingpub.com

Contents

Foreword

I am now 75, and most of my life has been devoted to a search for what might be called 'the mechanisms of the Peak Experience', or 'power consciousness'. This book might be regarded as a kind of DIY manual of how to achieve it.

Let me begin with an example of what I mean by 'power consciousness'. It concerns Blaise Pascal, and is from my book *Religion and the Rebel*:

> After a year of deteriorating health and spiritual
> uncertainty, Blaise Pascal had a vision. It was on the
> 23rd of November, 1654. At half past ten in the
> evening – probably as he lay in bed – an
> overpowering sense of health and vitality suddenly
> swept over him, a feeling of complete and total well-
> being; a certainty so sudden and complete that,
> when he wrote about it, he headed the page: fire.
> The sensation lasted for two hours, and he tried to
> capture it on paper. As he wrote, his feelings
> changed – no vision can be sustained for two hours
> – and he began to feel that he had sinned for the
> past few years. This is always the way with a vision.
> The first sensation is of vitality that makes one

affirm all existence, and love, love of the world, of its physical reality. As this certainty dies away, one becomes aware of the need for discipline if it is to be recaptured, and of one's lack of discipline in the past. Pascal's *Memorial* begins:

> fire
> God of Abraham, God of Isaac, God of Jacob,
>   not of the
> philosophers and scholars.
> Certitude, certitude, feeling, joy, peace.

Pascal sewed this account of his vision into his clothes, and carried it with him until his death.

Here is another example, from 'Vacillation' by W B Yeats:

> My fiftieth year had come and gone,
> I sat, a solitary man,
> In a crowded London shop,
> An open book and empty cup
> On the marble table-top.
>
> As on the shop and street I gazed
> My body of a sudden blazed;
> And twenty minutes more or less
> It seemed, so great my happiness,
> That I was blessèd and could bless.

Why did it happen? Yeats obviously had no idea. Neither have I. But I can pinpoint when I became actively involved in the subject.

Thirty-eight years ago, in 1969, I was asked to write a biography of the American psychologist Abraham Maslow. Maslow had first contacted me in the mid-1960s after reading a book of mine called *The Age of Defeat* (in America, *The Stature of Man*), in which I complained that throughout the 20th century, there has been a strong 'defeat-bias' in literature – 'You can't win' – due to what I called 'the fallacy of insignificance' – the feeling of most serious writers that life is a long-drawn-out defeat. (Or, as Sartre put it: 'It is meaningless that we live and meaningless that we die.') Only in children's stories and thrillers does the hero succeed in 'winning'.

Maslow told me he was excited by this because he also had a deep conviction that human nature has been 'sold short' by modern psychology – Freud in particular – and that we ought to take account of what he, Maslow, called 'higher ceilings of human nature'.

What fascinated me was Maslow's concept of the 'peak experience' (he called them PEs) – the experience of sudden overwhelming happiness, the feeling that life is wonderful; this, Maslow discovered, seems to happen to *healthy people* on a regular basis.

Here is a typical PE. A young mother was sitting watching her husband and children eating breakfast, when she was suddenly overwhelmed by a feeling of how much she loved them and how *lucky* she was: she went into the 'peak experience'.

But note this: she was lucky *before* she went into the peak experience. The peak experience simply involved *becoming aware* of how lucky she was. It really amounts to what G K Chesterton once called 'absurd good news' – a sudden sense of wonderful optimism about the future, the feeling that life is infinitely complex and infinitely exciting.

Moreover, Maslow discovered that when he talked to his students about peak experiences, they began remembering peak experiences that they had half forgotten about. For example, one young man was working his way through college as a jazz drummer, and he described how, at about two o'clock one morning, he began drumming so perfectly that *he couldn't do a thing wrong;* he went into the peak experience.

What was so interesting was that, as the students talked to one another every day about their peak experiences, *they began having peak experiences all the time.* It was obviously just a matter of feeling optimistic, and, so to speak, *reminding* themselves how good life was. (Later we shall see there is a more precise and more interesting explanation of why this happened.)

Now my first book *The Outsider* (1956) was also basically about peak experiences. It was a study of those Romantic poets and painters of the 19th century who experienced marvellous states of 'transcendent consciousness', moods in which it was self-evident that the whole universe was a wonderful place, so exciting that it seems absurd that anyone should ever want to die. Yet when they woke up the next morning, they would find themselves wondering what on earth they meant by it. It now seemed an illusion. Life was now self-evidently trivial and dull and ordinary, and it seemed grimly apparent that we are all *trapped* in this. This accounted for the despair that led to high levels of suicide and death by tuberculosis among such 'outsiders'.

These romantic outsiders seemed to feel that the world is a bad joke, a trap devised by the gods – that we long for the 'transcendent', yet always end by being forced to accept the everyday triviality, like children gulping down a nasty medicine. Yeats wrote in *The Shadowy Waters*:

> What the world's million lips are
>   searching for
> *Must* be substantial somewhere …

Yet no one seemed to have any idea how to find this 'other reality' – what I once called 'the other mode of consciousness'.

You don't have to be a romantic outsider to feel it. A musician friend told me how he had returned home one day feeling weary, and had poured himself a large whisky and put on a record of the baroque composer Praetorius – and had suddenly soared into ecstatic happiness – the 'other mode'. A BBC producer told me how he had been alone in an empty control room and played himself a record of the Schubert Octet, and had suddenly *become Schubert* – that is, he felt as if he was composing the music, and knew just why Schubert had written each bar. This experience is obviously what Sartre means when he remarked in *What is Literature* that to read a book with understanding is to rewrite it.

And now, here was Maslow suggesting that 'peak experiences' – glimpses of 'the other mode' – are perfectly natural to all healthy human beings. He also agreed with me that a large part of the problem is the sheer *negativity* of our culture, with pessimists like Graham Greene and Samuel Beckett assuring us that life is either meaningless or tragic. He felt that if the basically optimistic attitude that we shared could be brought to wider attention – grasped by large numbers of people – this stifling negativity would gradually disappear, and our culture would be transformed.

The reason I find the challenge so interesting is probably obvious. As a writer, I have spent my life engaged in thinking, and that thinking is essentially *connective*. *The Outsider* came to me on Christmas Day 1954 as a series of connections between figures as diverse as Sartre, Camus, Hemingway, Granville-Barker, T E Lawrence, Van Gogh, Tolstoy, Dostoevsky, William James, George Fox, Ramakrishna, Blake and Gurdjieff, and the book *flowed* from one to the other. It was an experience of excitement, with ideas tumbling over one another to get out.

This present book came to be written as a result of such an experience. One weekend in 1995, when my wife was away, I was visited by two friends, one of them an editor who was interested in commissioning a book about my ideas. For two days, insights poured out of me in a cascade. Early on Monday, my friends had to catch a train back to London, and as I drove them to the station I continued to add new connections that had occurred to me overnight. It was a beautiful, sunny morning, and as I drove back home, I felt that the first thing I wanted to do was to sit down at my computer and simply type for days. And when I did, this book took shape in 48 hours in the form of a 60-page outline. For various reasons this was pushed aside, and it is only now, 12 years later, that I have returned to it.

It seems to me that William James was describing the nature of thought itself when he said, in his 'A Suggestion About Mysticism', that mystical experience is not different *in kind* from ordinary consciousness, but is merely an extension of ordinary consciousness. After which he goes on to describe the basic 'connection experience': 'What happened each time was that I seemed all at once to be reminded of a past experience; and this reminiscence, ere I could conceive or name it distinctly, developed into something further that belonged with it, this in turn into something further still, and so on, until the process faded out, leaving me amazed at the sudden vision of increasing ranges of distant facts …'

The same experience is described in a book called *Megabrain* by Michael Hutchison. He is speaking of a brain-stimulator invented by the brain physiologist Joseph Light, who attached him to the machine in a restaurant. Unaware that it was switched on, Hutchison became increasingly excited:

> Yes, yes, I cried. I felt as if I were bursting at the
> seams. Full of wonder and excitement, I told Light
> some of my feelings about brain research. I told him
> about an article I was in the process of rewriting
> about the brain. I told him how I had become
> interested in the brain. At that moment a series of
> studies I had read about a variety of subjects,
> including the relation between protein synthesis and

> memory and the biochemical basis of addiction
> all flew together in my skull and I understood
> something new. Gesturing wildly and scribbling on
> a paper napkin, I began to explain my new insight
> … Suddenly I stopped, with my mouth hanging
> open in wild surmise. People seated in nearby
> booths were peering at me with great interest.
> 'Listen to me talk!' I said to Light. 'Jabbering like a
> wired-up monkey!'
>
> Light gave me a demonic grin and pointed his
> finger at the black gizmo on the table, and I realized
> that all this while subtle little electrical waves had
> been insinuating their way into my brain.

The machine had released into Hutchison's brain some of its natural opiates, the painkilling and euphoria-inducing endorphins. Light described to Hutchison how he had once driven 600 miles to a conference hooked up to his brain-stimulator, arrived full of energy and ideas, then later driven back without a break.

Now from *The Outsider* onward, I had stated my own conviction that *man is on the point of an evolutionary leap to a higher phase.* Moreover, I had come to feel that, in some paradoxical sense, we have already achieved this. But, like Maslow's young mother, who was 'lucky' before she was conscious of it, we are not yet *aware* of it.

I asked Maslow: 'Do you think we can learn to achieve the peak experience at will?' Maslow shook his head. 'No. They come when they want to and go when they want to. As far as I know, there is no infallible method for doing it.'

Now what he said seemed to me a blatant contradiction of his optimistic philosophy. The Romantics had also believed that the 'moments of vision' cannot be controlled. Pushkin compared the poet's heart to a coal which glows red when the wind of inspiration blows. But he cannot *make* it blow; he just has to sit and wait. This is precisely why the Romantics were so pessimistic. They felt passive and *helpless*.

Maslow's optimism implied there must be a way to make it happen at will. I set out to find this way. This book contains the essence of what I have discovered.

Chapter One

The Discovery of Inner Freedom

I disagreed with Maslow for a simple reason. I had noticed that if a crisis looms before us, then suddenly disappears, we are hurled into a state of happiness and optimism.

It was this discovery that turned Dostoevsky into a great writer. As a young man (the author of *Poor Folk*) he was touchy and paranoid. Then, along with several associates, he was arrested as a revolutionary and sentenced to death. In front of the firing squad, with three minutes to live, he divided his time into three one-minute periods: one to think about the past, one to contemplate the present, one to think about the future. And at that point, a messenger rode up with a pardon for the condemned men. Dostoevsky never forgot that 'crisis vision' – the recognition that the world is an incredibly beautiful place, and that we are prevented from seeing this mainly by laziness, negativity and force of habit.

Now the Romantics of the 19th century, about whom I had written in *The Outsider*, had also glimpsed this truth. So why did so many of them commit suicide, or die of alcoholism or some obviously self-induced illness?

Let us begin by looking more closely at these Romantics. Literary historians agree that the starting point of Romanticism was Goethe's novel *The Sorrows of Young Werther* (1774) about a young painter who – at the beginning of the book – is staying in a village among the mountains, and finds his surroundings enchanting. Later he falls in love, is disappointed, and commits suicide – but in a sense, all that is less important than that initial sense of wonder and delight. For it is self-evident that the reason Werther responds so deeply to the mountains is that *he sees in them a reflection of his own inner power, his own inner mountain landscape.* He is possessed by an intuition that man is far bigger than he thinks he is: in fact, that in some obscure sense, he is a god.

What is so hard for us to grasp is that Goethe was one of the first to realize that nature is beautiful. This sounds absurd. Yet the previous generation of English writers – Pope and Swift and Dr Johnson – had found nature rather boring; Johnson took a tour of the Hebrides in the year *Werther* came out, and found that it made him long to be back in London. Pope's idea of nature was a well-designed formal garden, and his lines: 'Know then thyself; presume not God to scan/The proper study of mankind is man'(An Essay on Man: Epistle II) expressed his feeling that man is a creature of *this* world, and had bloody well better make the best of it. And here, suddenly, were Goethe and Wordsworth and Blake going into ecstasies at the sight of mountains and sunsets.

Now in the year 1740, a printer called Samuel Richardson wrote a novel called *Pamela*, which is about a servant girl of that name whose master is determined to seduce her, but is so touched by her goodness that he marries her instead. This was the first novel in our modern European sense of the word, and readers bit their nails as the wicked squire leapt out of a cupboard and threw her on the bed. *Pamela* swept across Europe and became the first best-selling novel. Moreover, it turned England into a 'nation of readers'. (Lending libraries sprang up soon afterwards solely to supply the ravenous demand for imitations of *Pamela*.) Before Richardson, the big family outing of the week was going to church on Sunday to hear the sermon – because sermons 'took you out of yourself'. (And, incredibly, volumes of sermons often became bestsellers.) *Pamela* was really a soap opera about the girl next door; the reader could identify with her, and fly away on a kind of magic carpet. *Pamela* taught European man (and, more important, woman) to *dream*, to use the imagination. It was *Pamela* – and its successors – that caused that immense change from the down-to-earth age of Dr Johnson to the Romantic age of Goethe and Byron.

But did the novel really cause such a change? Why was it such a revolution?

The answer is that it started a phase of modern history that might be called *the discovery of inner freedom*.

Let us try to get inside the head of a man like Dr Johnson, and understand how he saw himself. First, he was a Christian, who took it for granted that he was a poor sinner who would one day die and face judgement (he was terrified of death). Oddly enough, he had also glimpsed the same revelation as Dostoevsky, as he reveals in his comment: 'When a man knows he is to be hanged in a fortnight, it concentrates his mind wonderfully.' In other words, he saw that our major problem is a kind of mental *diffuseness,* and that what we need is to be concentrated. Yet he never tried to pursue this insight to its conclusion.

Why? Because he had no sense of possessing an 'inner mountain landscape'. As far as he was concerned, he was just plain down-to-earth Sam Johnson. And this was typical of the 18th-century spirit of the age. The philosopher David Hume argued that man does not possess an 'inner self'. He said that when he looked inside himself, he did not see the essential David Hume, but merely a lot of ideas and impressions blowing around like leaves in the wind. Free will is an illusion. Descartes had said: 'I think therefore I am.' According to Hume, that is untrue. You don't 'think' – you merely 'free-associate' – one thought or feeling leading *automatically* to another. This philosophy was most clearly expressed by the French rationalist La Mettrie in a book called *Man the Machine* (1748), of which I shall have more to say.

Dr Johnson, of course, would have rejected this with horror. So how did he see himself – the essential Sam Johnson? Well, he would have said that, inside his body, there was a soul. And if you had asked him how he 'saw' his soul, he would probably have replied: 'A kind of sphere' – for this is how the philosopher Leibniz saw souls: not as identical spheres, but as individual spheres, each quite unlike every other. (He called them 'monads'.)

In short, the soul is shaped like a football. But according to the sceptical philosophers, it differs from a football in one important respect. A football has an inner bladder which inflates. Leibniz's picture of the soul was more like a 'bladderless' football; a simple leather sphere with nothing inside it, like a tubeless tyre. That is how Dr Johnson would have seen his soul.

That image enables us to understand the change that came about in the Romantic age. For Romantic footballs did have bladders inside them. And those bladders could not only expand with a feeling of ecstasy, but could also contract, with a kind of hiss of air, into a sense of deep peace and relaxation.

This also enables us to understand the vast gulf that yawns between the rationalist idea of the soul, and the Romantic view.

Young Werther experienced a marvellous sense of peace and ecstasy as he contemplated the mountains. His *everyday self* suddenly became totally unimportant. It was as if the bladder inside the football had contracted, so there was now a one-inch gap between the leather football and the bladder inside. *And the bladder could suddenly move freely.* That is the essence of Romanticism: that sense of inner-freedom, that feeling that 'you' and your personality are not at all the same thing. And in that important sense, the Romantics were not at all like down-to-earth Dr Johnson.

This football image may sound far-fetched, but it expresses precisely what the Romantics felt. The triviality of everyday life, with its problems and responsibilities, destroys our inner freedom. In fact, most people don't even realize they possess this inner freedom, this ability to relax inside the football and explore an inner world. They think they *are* the football.

So what the Romantics realized – instinctively – was that they possessed *an outer being and an inner being*. We are not usually aware of this inner-being, because it is pressed too tightly against the football. But as soon as we relax, we make the discovery of inner freedom.

Now it was *Pamela* that first made huge numbers of people recognize that they possessed inner-freedom. This was not, of course, the first time in history – Plato's *Symposium* makes it obvious that he knew it too, when Socrates explains that true love of beauty surpasses mere physical objects, and focuses upon the ultimate beauty of love itself. But *Pamela* enabled farmers' wives and vicars' daughters to feel it too.

Think what happens when you are lying in bed on a freezing winter morning, and you have to get up in ten minutes. The bed has never seemed so warm and delicious. Yet on a Sunday, when you can stay in bed as long as you like, you can never revive that marvellous sense of warmth. Why? Because when you know you have to get up in ten minutes, you *relax* in order to appreciate the warmth. The 'inner being' separates from the outside of the football and you feel freedom. On a Sunday, you feel: 'I am free to do what I like,' so you don't make that effort of relaxation which turns freedom into a reality.

Another way of putting the same thing. When you are in a 'practical' frame of mind, you see life from a worm's eye view, as if you are lying on the floor looking upward. When you relax deeply, you are able to see life from a bird's eye view, like an eagle hovering in the sky.

Here is a vital insight. When you are stuck in the 'worm's eye view', you are also stuck in the present moment, the 'here-and-now'. I call this 'mono-consciousness'. But think what happens when a child sits in front of the fire on Christmas Eve, with the wind howling and the snow pattering against the windows. He is in *two places at once.* He is there, in the room, but he can enjoy it because a part of him is outside in the snow. He is in 'duo-consciousness'. Men are only truly happy and free when they are in duo-consciousness. This is why you enjoy bed so much on a freezing winter morning.

Now we can begin to understand the problem that caused the high rate of suicides and alcoholism in the 19th century.

The Romantic poet did not feel he belonged in this boring, practical world. He felt that he was, in some profound sense, a god. Yet everything about the real world seemed to contradict it. Worse still, his proneness to retreat into a world of dreams left him enfeebled, unable to face the real world. Yeats was honest enough to admit in his *Memoirs* (page 125) that he masturbated himself into a state of exhaustion in those early days when he was writing poems about fairyland.

> Come away O human child
> To the waters and the wild
> With a fairy hand in hand
> For the world's more full of weeping than
>   you can understand ...

> 'The Stolen Child'

This makes another central point. Maslow pointed out that most 'peakers' are healthy, practical people. In my book on Maslow, *New Pathways in Psychology*, I expressed the problem by saying that human beings are like cars, who need to be driven regularly to keep their batteries charged. When we stagnate, the batteries go flat, and we experience the main problem of the 19th-century Romantics: *life failure.* Auden wrote:

> Put the car away; when life fails
> What's the good of going to Wales?

> **'It's No Use Raising a Shout'**

Life failure is caused by allowing your vital batteries to get too low.

That explains why the discovery of inner freedom had such disastrous results for the Romantics: it prevented them from adjusting to the real world.

The essential problem of the Romantics was what I once called 'the Bombard effect', after the Frenchman Alain Bombard, who recounts in *The Bombard Story* how he sailed a dinghy across the Atlantic, living on squashed fish and plankton, to prove that ship-wrecked mariners did not have to die of starvation. Halfway across the Atlantic, he was spotted by a ship that persuaded him to come on board and eat a normal breakfast. It nearly killed him, for when he went back to his squashed fish and plankton, he vomited for days before his stomach readjusted. The Romantics found them-selves unable to adjust to the squashed fish and plankton of ordinary existence after their vision of ecstasy and romance …

The problem of the 19th century is symbolized by Van Gogh. When you look at a painting like *The Starry Night*, you can see that it is about power consciousness – that explosion of sheer affirmation and vitality. Yet Van Gogh committed suicide, leaving behind a note that read: 'Misery will never end.' Which was true: *The Starry Night* or the suicide note? This was the central problem I posed in *The Outsider*. Carlyle called it 'Eternal Yes versus Eternal No'. Even Cezanne can be seen to be about 'power consciousness'. His strangely geometrical rocks and trees are saying: 'This is how I see reality. Never mind your messy, chaotic everyday reality – I am imposing *my* vision on reality to show you what it ought to be like.' Nietzsche, of course, with his 'will to power' (which, I must emphasize, should not be associated with Nazism – Nietzsche loathed anti-semites as brainless idiots) is the very essence of this new 'power consciousness'. Yet after giving it its supreme expression in *Thus Spoke Zarathustra* (which he said is about 'great health') he died insane.

So we come to the end of the 19th century, with its 'tragic generation' of the 1890s, poets like Dowson and Verlaine, painters like Aubrey Beardsley and Sickert and Whistler. Dowson wrote:

> The fire is out, and spent the warmth thereof,
> This is the end of every song man sings.

'Dregs'

The work of these artists and poets is permeated by sadness, a feeling of: 'You can't win'. And this becomes almost the theme song of the 20th century, the age of defeat.

This brings us to the problem that I have labelled 'the Ecclesiastes effect'.

Chapter Two

The Ecclesiastes Effect

When I was a teenager, I spent a great deal of time in a state of boredom. The boredom caused my energies to sink. And when your energies are low, you feel that nothing is worth the effort.

I realized that this was bad for me, and often forced myself to make an effort – going for a cycle ride, or a walk in the park, or to the local library. In spite of which, I often felt a complete lack of motivation. It was so bad that if I paused as I walked along the street, I could see no reason to start walking again. I felt stuck in the present, like a fly trapped on sticky flypaper. I also spent a great deal of time engaged in sexual fantasy. But of course, masturbation only depleted my energies further.

It seemed to me that the prophet Ecclesiastes had recognized the truth about human existence when he said: 'Vanity of vanities, all is vanity'. Obviously, I felt, Ecclesiastes also spent most of his life in a state of boredom and depression.

I came upon a book called *The Varieties of Religious Experience* by William James, and in this I found a chapter that seemed to describe my own condition. It was called 'The Sick Soul'. It followed immediately on a chapter called 'The Religion of Healthy-Mindedness', which speaks of 'people who have been born with a bottle or two of champagne to their credit', and others who can easily be pushed into a state of tension and anxiety. James introduces the word 'threshold' to indicate our level of sensitivity – for example, a person with a low noise threshold can be awakened by the slightest noise, whereas one with a high noise threshold can sleep through the most tremendous racket. Similarly, some people have a high pain threshold which means that low levels of pain do not bother them, while others have such a low pain threshold that even reading about another's pain makes them feel depressed. Anyone who has read *Crime and Punishment* can see that Dostoevsky, like his hero Raskolnikov, had an extremely low pain threshold, and was always being plunged into misery by the sight of suffering.

It seemed to me that the type of persons I called 'Outsiders' were people with such a low pain threshold that they were always on the verge of plunging into despair, and that when Vincent Van Gogh committed suicide after leaving a note that read: 'Misery will never end', he was protesting about the pain of life. And in *The Brothers Karamazov*, Ivan tells his gentle younger brother: 'It's not God I reject, Alyosha. But I just want to give him back his entrance ticket.'

When I started to write my first book, *The Outsider,* it was my original plan to call it *The Pain Threshold.*

William James was well qualified to write about the pain threshold, for one of the most striking cases he discusses was actually his own, although he claims that he had translated it from the French of a correspondent:

> Whilst in this state of philosophic pessimism and general depression of spirits about my prospects, I went one evening into a dressing-room in the twilight to procure some article that was there; when suddenly there fell upon me without any warning, just as if it came out of the darkness, a horrible fear of my own existence. Simultaneously there arose in my mind the image of an epileptic patient whom I had seen in the asylum, a black-haired youth with greenish skin, entirely idiotic, who used to sit all day on one of the benches, or rather shelves against the wall, with his knees drawn up against his chin, and the coarse gray undershirt, which was his only garment, drawn over them inclosing his entire figure. He sat there like a sort of sculptured Egyptian cat or Peruvian mummy, moving nothing but his black eyes and looking absolutely non-human. This image and my fear entered into a species of combination with each other. That shape am I, I felt, potentially. Nothing that I possess can defend me against that fate, if the hour for it should strike for me as it struck for him. There was such a horror of him, and such a perception of my own merely momentary discrepancy from him, that it was as if something hitherto solid within my breast

gave way entirely, and I became a mass of quivering fear. After this the universe was changed for me altogether. I awoke morning after morning with a horrible dread at the pit of my stomach, and with a sense of the insecurity of life that I never knew before, and that I have never felt since. It was like a revelation; and although the immediate feelings passed away, the experience has made me sympathetic with the morbid feelings of others ever since. It gradually faded, but for months I was unable to go out into the dark alone.

In general I dreaded to be left alone. I remember wondering how other people could live, how I myself had ever lived, unconscious of that pit of insecurity beneath the surface of life. My mother in particular, a very cheerful person, seemed to me a perfect paradox in her unconsciousness of danger, which you may well believe I was very careful not to disturb by revelations of my own state of mind.

Having been through similar experiences, I am able to say exactly what happened to James. Depression causes our energies to sink until we feel defenceless. In this state, a frightening mental image, like James's catatonic patient, produces paralysing fear, a sense of total vulnerability. And this is why he found his mother, 'a very cheerful person', so hard to understand. In fact, in this state, it seems that the whole human race is blissfully unaware of the danger that lurks beneath its feet. It seems perfectly obvious what Ecclesiastes meant when he said 'All is vanity'.

Interestingly enough, James had succeeded in throwing off his depression by reading a comment by the French philosopher Charles Renouvier. The latter had remarked that once we have convinced ourselves that free will does not exist, it is hard to think of anything to disprove this. If we are nothing more than penny-in-the-slot machines, then anything we do or say has a motive – to prove we are free – and therefore is not a truly free choice. But Renouvier pointed out that *I can sustain a thought when I could just as easily think of something else*, and that this proves I am free. James brooded on this argument, and concluded that it was true: I *can* decide what to think about next, and change the direction of my thought as often as I choose. Therefore I have freedom of choice. The moment James became convinced of this, he began to throw off his depression.

We can see the immense importance of believing in the reality of free will. As soon as James had found a reason to accept the reality of free will, he had found a reason to feel optimistic. And that optimism made the difference between mental health and sickness.

Maslow describes a case that makes the same point. One of his early patients was a girl who was suffering from such deep depression that she had even ceased to menstruate. It soon emerged that the problem was job-frustration. She had been a bright student at college, and hoped to take a degree in sociology. Then came the slump of the 1930s, and she was suddenly the only one in her family with a job, and was supporting the rest of them. She was working as a personnel manageress in a chewing gum factory. Soon the boredom had soaked through to her bones, so she ceased to take any pleasure in her daily routine.

Instead of seeking some Freudian solution, Maslow said: 'Why don't you just study sociology at night school?' It worked, and the girl was soon enjoying life again. Maslow's solution was based on the recognition that intelligent people have a need to use their intelligence creatively, and that failure to do this can lead to frustration and such inappropriate solutions as alcoholism or drug use.

The lesson is that boredom and lack of purpose are among the most destructive states we can experience.

What is the general solution to this problem of the Ecclesiastes effect? The problem might be compared to what happens if you leave a car in the garage all winter: the battery tends to go flat. To prevent this happening is perfectly easy. You take the car out for a run periodically, or occasionally recharge it with a battery charger.

The mind responds to similar treatment. The narrator of Hermann Hesse's novel *Journey to the East* puts his finger on it when he says: 'I, whose calling was really only that of a violinist and story-teller, was responsible for the provision of music for our group, and I then discovered how a long time devoted to small details exalts us and increases our strength.'

The same point emerges in an anecdote of the Zen master Ikkyu. A workman asked Ikkyu to write something on his slate, and Ikkyu wrote: 'Attention!' Disappointed, the workman asked him to write something else, and Ikkyu wrote: 'Attention, attention!' 'What does attention mean?' asked the workman, and Ikkyu replied, 'Attention means attention.'

T E Lawrence was making the same point when he said: 'Happiness is absorption.' He had noted that attention to small details induces absorption, a kind of warm inner glow.

The complexities of living exhaust our attention and cause a leakage of energy, and the leakage drains our vital batteries. When Maslow told his patient to study sociology at night school, he was advising her to seek out something that would absorb her attention, and halt the drain on her battery.

In daily life, anything that 'grabs the attention' has the automatic effect of focusing our energy. For most of us, one of the commonest causes is sexual stimulation, the subject of the chapter that follows.

Chapter Three

The Sexual Explosion

My first book *The Outsider* opens with a quotation from a novel by Henri Barbusse, called *L'Enfer* (*Hell*).

> In the air, on top of a tram, a girl is sitting. Her dress, lifted a little, blows out. But a block in the traffic separates us. The tramcar glides away, fading like a nightmare.
>
> Moving in both directions, the street is full of dresses which sway, offering themselves airily, the skirts lifting; dresses that lift and yet do not lift.
>
> In the tall and narrow shop mirror I see myself approaching, rather pale and heavy-eyed. It is not a woman I want – it is all women, and I seek for them in those around me, one by one …

It catches with precision the reaction of a male whose attention is suddenly focused by a woman's skirt lifting in the breeze. Then something blocks his view and he watches in frustration as the tramcar moves away. The Paris street is full of swaying dresses that offer tantalizing glimpses (in 1908 an ankle would have been enough to cause excitement). And the nameless hero adds gloomily: 'It is not a woman I want – it is all women …'. But when, a few minutes later, he picks up a prostitute and returns to her room, the craving remains unsatisfied, and he feels as frustrated as ever. For the craving for sex is not purely physical, like an empty stomach; when he says he wants 'all women', he is speaking of the eternal feminine.

This is why human beings find sex so alluring, for it is also basically a romantic impulse; it offers a glimpse of 'the eternal longing'.

But Roy Hazelwood, a member of the FBI's 'criminal profiling' unit, whose task involves trapping sex killers, has made this important remark: 'Sex crime is not about sex – it's about power.' We could generalize and say that sex is about power consciousness. This is why Barbusse's narrator gains little satisfaction from a prostitute. The transaction is purely commercial; it involves neither romance nor power.

Five years after *Pamela* came out in 1740, John Cleland's *Fanny Hill* was published – the first truly 'pornographic novel'. (One Frenchman called pornography 'Books that one reads with one hand'.) No sooner had western man started to learn about the world of imagination than he began to use it for sexual fantasy. The Gothic novels – like Matthew Lewis's *The Monk* – which would become so popular a few years later were full of rape and violation.

There is surely an odd significance in the fact that the Marquis de Sade, the patron saint of sexual perversion, was born in 1740, the year *Pamela* appeared.

What was happening is interesting. The problem with the Romantics is that they didn't know how to *canalize* these volcanic energies from the depths of the psyche. Faced with the awesome spectacle of a mountain by moonlight, Wordsworth confessed that he was filled with a sense of 'unknown modes of being'. Yet he couldn't *summon* those modes of being at will. The best he could do was summon a little gentle melancholy in a poem about daffodils 'through recollection in solitude'.

Sade and his followers (pornography became a kind of industry around 1820) chose a cruder method. They summoned sexual energy through coarse fantasy, and canalized it through *the sense of forbiddenness*. But compared to the true romantic ecstasy, this volcanic sexual energy was like methylated spirit compared to a fine claret. And its effects were as disastrous. It gave its readers a temporary feeling of direction, which soon evaporated, leaving behind a sense of futility. So the fantasy had to be made cruder still – more violent and 'forbidden'. Sade's *120 Days of Sodom* ends with absurd visions of shooting pregnant women out of cannons. This was an example of the law of diminishing returns. Yet this *was* one of the major routes chosen by the instinctive 'quest for power consciousness' in the 19th century.

By 1880, Richard von Krafft-Ebing was astonished by the proliferation of extraordinary sexual perversions which he described in his *Psychopathia Sexualis*. And even the modern reader is taken aback by the perversions that he lists, such as a man who placed leeches in his mistress's vagina, one who paid prostitutes to allow him to defecate in their mouths, and one who could only achieve orgasm when drinking a girl's blood. It is true that many of these patients came from families suffering from mental 'degeneration', but a few decades later, the majority of the cases described by the Berlin psychiatrist Magnus Hirschfeld in *Sexual Disasters* (1926) seem to involve people who are otherwise fairly normal. It would seem that this cascade of sexual oddities was one of the consequences of the spirit of Romanticism, and its effect upon those suffering from sexual frustration.

In other words, the full significance of the 'sexual explosion' lies in its imaginative dimension. Animal sex depends on the smell of the female on heat. Over the past half million years, human sex has come to depend increasingly on visual stimulus. But there is another major difference between man and our nearest relative the monkey. Although male monkeys engage in genital play, they do not masturbate in our human sense of the word. For that they need the stimulus of a female.

Now in most departments, our human imagination is feeble. For example, you can imagine trapping your fingers in a door, and wince at the thought. But it doesn't actually hurt your fingers. Or you can imagine eating when you are hungry, but it doesn't make you feel less hungry. Sex is the one department in which you can indulge in fantasy, *and carry it through to its logical conclusion* – orgasm. There is a sense in which masturbation is the highest faculty yet developed by man.

But this is not my main concern. I am suggesting that sexual fantasy can achieve such extraordinary intensity because it can call upon the energies of the unconscious mind, and that the next step in human evolution will enable us to bring the same intensity to *all* fantasy. This will involve the development of what I call

'Faculty X' – a concept I shall explain more fully in chapter eleven.

The sexual explosion had another unforeseen consequence: social revolution. This was due almost entirely to the influence of one man: Jean Jacques Rousseau, whose novel *La Nouvelle Heloise* (1761) was published two decades after Richardson's *Pamela*, and achieved even greater popularity.

The New Heloise tells the story of St Preux, a penniless young tutor who falls in love with his beautiful pupil Julie, who becomes his mistress. Rousseau argues that if two people are in love, then they have a right to become lovers. In 1761, this attitude caused shock all over Europe, since a girl's virginity was regarded as the property of her future husband – and a valuable asset in acquiring one.

Nowadays Rousseau is remembered mainly as the author of *The Social Contract*, with its famous opening sentence: 'Man is born free and is everywhere in chains' – which, it could be argued, led directly to the French Revolution. But *The Social Contract* appeared two years after *The New Heloise*, and it could be said that Rousseau's doctrine of social freedom sprang out of his doctrine of sexual freedom. Rousseau would become the progenitor of a whole line of social revolutionaries from Proudhon to Karl Marx.

This recognition sounds an ominous note, as we recall that both the French Revolution and the Russian Revolution quickly turned into bloodshed and tyranny. Rousseau's vision of an ideal society ended in the guillotine; Marx's dream of a just society led to Stalin and Mao. And this was not an unfortunate accident of history. The bloodshed was already inherent in the dream of

Rousseau and Marx because they were unrealistic. They left out of account the fact that human beings are subject to boredom. Every schoolboy knows that feeling of delight on the first day of a holiday, and how quickly it turns into habit. The German philosopher Fichte made this observation when he said: 'To be free is nothing; to *become* free is heavenly.' That is because when we suddenly become free, the freedom is a pleasant shock. But it is soon taken for granted and becomes mechanical. We are still free in the physical sense; but the sensation of freedom has vanished.

This applies even more so to the vision of sexual freedom. Sex is one of the most effective means we have of creating 'the flow experience'. This useful term was coined in the 1970s by Mihalyi Csikczentmihalyi, a psychologist at the University of Chicago, who examined groups as diverse as musical composers, surgeons, Japanese motorcycle gangs, rock climbers and devotees of ocean cruising, and found the same common denominator: the experience of energy flowing smoothly and powerfully, producing a kind of ecstasy. He concluded that all such activities are ways for people to 'test the limits of their being, and to transcend their former conception of self by extending skills and undergoing new experiences'.

Maslow called such persons 'self-actualizers'. They are driven by an urge to evolve.

The flow experience is also what Maslow meant by the peak experience, but the word 'flow' is more evocative, suggesting the ongoing movement of music. Flow is the opposite of stagnation and boredom. William James speaks of a football player who plays the game *technically* perfectly; and then one day, he is taken over by the excitement of play, and suddenly *the game is playing him*. This is the essence of the flow experience. It is evolution in action: we can *feel* ourselves evolving.

Our energies could be compared to a river flowing over a plain. If the flow is too slow, the river begins to meander, as it accumulates silt and mud. In this state, we long for the flow experience, the equivalent of a violent storm in the hills that will send a roaring torrent to sweep away the mud and straighten out the bends.

This enables us to understand the psychology of sex crime. Sex criminals tend to be young – in their twenties – so a sudden sexual stimulus, like seeing a girl bending over in a miniskirt, arouses violent desire. Ted Bundy, an American serial killer (executed 1989) described how he had been passing a student rooming hostel when he saw a girl undressing. From then on, he 'made a project' of hanging around women's hostels at dusk. In spite of guilt and shame, he continued to do this until one day he found a door open, went into the bedroom, and bludgeoned a sleeping student – the first of at least 40 attacks. We can see why Bundy felt he was pursuing the key to his personal evolution; rape was a method of inducing instant 'flash floods'. After kidnapping a girl and driving her to some spot where he could rape her at leisure, it is clear that Bundy would experience 'power consciousness' just as surely if he had turned into Beethoven, Goethe or Napoleon.

The unconscious assumption of the sex criminal is an obscure conviction that if he does it often enough, it will sweep away some kind of inner barrier and turn him into a kind of superman.

This is what makes the idea so dangerous. Even a writer as intelligent and morally perceptive as Dostoevsky planned to

33

write a novel called *The Life of a Great Sinner*, in which the central character would literally sin his way to salvation (i.e. self-actualization). We can see that Dostoevsky felt that 'sin' ('the 'forbidden') could, in theory, intensify the flow experience, while failing to grasp that most of us have an instinctive inhibition against causing pain. But this is clearly why the novel remained unfinished. His attempts to write it ran up against his natural gentleness and kindness.

This disturbing connection between crime and the flow experience has been around for a long time. Even before the novels of the Marquis de Sade, whose central argument is that *nothing* should be forbidden, Friedrich Schiller's play *The Robbers* (1778) had outraged Germany, with its hero who joins a band of brigands that storms cities, robs treasuries and violates nunneries. Schiller's Karl Moor declares: 'Law has never produced a man of true grandeur. It is freedom that incubates the colossal and the extreme.' A German military man commented: 'If God had known Schiller would write *The Robbers* he would not have created the world.'

It is slightly alarming to realize that many perfectly respectable philosophers have been saying the same kind of thing for the past two centuries. William Blake remarked: 'Rather murder an infant in its cradle than nurse unacted desire.' Henrik Ibsen caused a scandal with *A Doll's House* when he made the heroine walk out on her husband and children, declaring that the need for self-development was more important than obeying the rules of conventional morality. Undershaft, the armaments manufacturer in George Bernard Shaw's *Major Barbara*, justifies himself with the statement: 'I moralised and starved until one day I swore I would be a full-fed free man at all costs; that nothing should stop me except a bullet, neither reason nor morals nor the lives of other men. I said "Thou shalt starve ere I starve"; and with that word I became free and great. I was a dangerous man until I had my will: now I am a useful, beneficent, kindly person.' He has, so to speak, sinned his way to salvation. Elsewhere in the play he explains that morality is relative: 'For me there is only one true morality, but it might not fit you, as you do not manufacture aerial battleships …'

In *Civilization and Its Discontents*, Sigmund Freud argues that man has created a civilization that has turned into a prison; it demands that he constantly repress desires that are natural to animals in the wild. Unlike Ibsen and Shaw, he is not arguing that we should cast off conventional morality; his purpose is simply to explain why our society is so riddled with neurosis. But Freud's argument could also be regarded as a justification for seeking the 'flow experience' at all costs.

When William Blake wrote *The Marriage of Heaven and Hell* there were no criminals capable of adopting his suggestions – he lived in the age of footpads and highwaymen. And when Ibsen wrote in his journal: 'Liberation consists in securing for individuals the right to free themselves, each according to his particular need', there were no sex criminals to quote him as an excuse for rape. It was in the 1880s, when anarchists began to plant bombs on the grounds that all power is corrupt, that it gradually became clear that there is a negative side to individual self-development. Yet even *Major Barbara*, written in 1905, belongs to the 'age of innocence' when criminals were more concerned with burglary and petty theft than heroic rebellion. It would be more than four decades before an American serial killer named Melvin Rees would declare: 'You can't say it's wrong to kill – only individual standards make it right or wrong,' and demonstrate that Undershaft's relativist morality could be used to justify rape and murder.

In 1845, Max Stirner's *Der Einziger und sein Eigentum* (*Ego and His Own*) asserted the importance of the individual ego in the face of all philosophies that try to reduce him to a member of the crowd – or the State or the Church – and that man is incapable of real altruism because he is, whether he likes it or not, a lone ego whose own interests come first. It is because this loneliness frightens him that he loves feeling himself to be a part of a group or a mob – anything to avoid the burden of standing alone. Sadly, the book failed to arouse much interest, and ten years later Stirner died, poor and forgotten.

By then, Nietzsche was already carrying the banner of lonely individualism, and in 1887 he worked out its consequences in one of the most frightening books of the 19th century, *Towards a Genealogy of Morals,* subtitled 'An Attack'.

It is, in some ways, Nietzsche's most shocking book, the one in which he develops the dubious contrast between 'master morality' and 'slave morality'.

He begins by asking: what is the basis of our idea of good and evil? Where does the idea of goodness originate? Studying its development in ancient languages, Nietzsche reached the conclusion that 'good' originally meant 'noble' and that 'evil' originally meant 'common', 'plebian', or 'base'.

To begin with, he says, the nobles were a priestly caste, so 'good' and 'noble' meant the same thing. Then (and here he is historically correct, as I discovered when I came to write *A Criminal History of Mankind*) soldiers and world conquerors came on the scene, and became an independent power in society. The soldier's idea of good remained an ideal of chivalry, aristocracy and nobility. This meant that the priests began to develop their own rival notion of good – involving intelligence, spirituality, self-sacrifice, and so on. All this came to a head in the religious philosophy of Judaism.

> Whatever else has been done to damage the powerful and great of this earth seems trivial compared to what the Jews have done, that priestly people who succeeded in avenging themselves on their enemies and oppressors by radically inverting all their values … This was a strategy entirely appropriate to a priestly people whose vindictiveness had gone most deeply underground. It was the Jew who, with frightening consistency, dared to invert all the aristocratic value-equations – good, noble, powerful, beautiful, happy, favoured-of-the gods – and maintain, with the furious hatred of the underprivileged and impotent, that 'only the poor, the powerless, are good; only the suffering, sick and ugly, truly blessed.'

And so, says Nietzsche, man became prey to 'bad conscience', and has built his culture on an appalling inversion of all genuine and healthy values.

Now before we take the easy way out and denounce Nietzsche (as Bertrand Russell did) as a mad messiah, a sick anti-semite, a proto-Nazi, we have to recognize that he also detested anti-semites as brainless idiots, and that he would probably have reacted to Hitler with the same aristocratic disdain as Oswald Spengler, who earned the Fuhrer's anger by saying that he was less of a hero (*helden*) than a heroic tenor (*heldentenor* – the tenor who sings the lead in most Wagner operas). No one who has read *Thus Spoke Zarathustra* can reduce Nietzsche to a mad messiah. His starting point was his own profound sense of the inadequacy of most human beings. We may reply that this was Nietzsche's bad luck. He happened to be what modern zoologists call an 'alpha', a high-dominance male, a member of a very tiny percentage of any animal group; he was also perhaps the most intelligent man of his age. So it was quite inevitable that he should feel superior to most people he met – as inevitable as a beautiful woman knowing herself to be more beautiful than other women. What good could it do him to bang his head against a brick wall of zoological reality?

Nietzsche's answer to that question was that even fairly mediocre human beings could be less mediocre if they were not enslaved by stupid values. Let us, he said, stop glorifying these Jewish (and Christian) values, and recognize that they have been elevated by a kind of conspiracy of the mediocre and ignoble. That, at least, would be a beginning.

History tells us that it would *not* be a very good beginning. Even before the rise of Adolf Hitler, two Chicago students named Nathan Leopold and Richard Loeb, both deeply influenced by Nietzsche, decided to commit 'the perfect murder' to prove to one another that they were supermen. The victim, chosen almost at random, was a 14-year-old named Bobby Franks. He was lured into a hired car and battered to death, but Leopold's spectacles were found close to the body; the pair confessed and only narrowly avoided the death penalty.

It was in the late 1950s that the 28-year-old jazz pianist named Melvin Rees – mentioned earlier – committed nine murders motivated by sex, in one case kidnapping a family of four out for an afternoon drive and then violating the wife and four-year-old daughter. He was caught after a tip-off from a friend, to whom he had remarked, in the true spirit of de Sade: 'You can't say it's wrong to kill – only individual standards make it right or wrong.' He was sentenced to death but reprieved.

Ian Brady, the British 'Moors Murderer' of the 1960s, was also motivated by Nietzschean philosophy and admiration of the Marquis de Sade. Like Sade, he believed that the Christian morality that forbids killing was a case of 'slave morality' with no logical rationale. Brady and his mistress Myra Hindley killed five children, whom Brady raped. I came to know him well, over a correspondence that lasted for nine years, and was even instrumental in finding a publisher for a book he wrote, in which he argued, like Melvin Rees, that only individual standards make killing right or wrong. But I found Brady's most significant comment to be one he made to a journalist when speaking of the five murders: 'I felt old at 26. Everything was ashes. I felt there was nothing of interest

– nothing to hook myself on to. I had experienced everything.' In other words, giving full rein to his violent impulses had produced the Ecclesiastes effect. And, as we have noted, the Ecclesiastes effect is the result of allowing our vital batteries to run down.

A similar observation was made by Joel Norris, a psychiatrist who studied the case of Leonard Lake, one of the most horrific serial killers of the 1980s. Inspired by *The Collector*, a novel by John Fowles about a man who kidnaps and imprisons a girl, Lake and his associate Charles Ng kidnapped many women and held them as 'sex slaves', murdering them when they tired of them. The remains of 26 bodies were found buried on his farm at Calaveras County, California. Lake recorded the crimes on videotapes and in his journals, and Norris commented (in his book *The Menace of the Serial Killer*):

> His dreams of success had eluded him, he admitted to
> himself that his boasts about heroic deeds in Vietnam
> were all delusions, and the increasing number of
> victims he was burying in the trench behind his
> bunker only added to his unhappiness. By the time
> he was arrested in San Francisco, Lake had reached
> the final stage of the serial murderer syndrome:
> he realized that he had come to a dead end with
> nothing but his own misery to show for it.

Like Brady's remark about feeling old at 26, this reveals the fallacy behind Rousseau's philosophy of sexual freedom. Several times in his correspondence with me, Brady had remarked,

'I've done everything,' rather as a glutton might say, 'I've eaten everything,' and wonder why he had indigestion. It reveals the passive attitude to experience that engenders the Ecclesiastes effect, and the failure to grasp what T E Lawrence meant by 'happiness is absorption'.

Which explains why, in the final analysis, Rousseau's dreams of sexual liberty, like his views of political liberty, fail to reflect the reality of the human situation.

Chapter Four

What is Cosmic Consciousness?

In 1901, a British doctor named Richard Maurice Bucke published one of the classics of mysticism, *Cosmic Consciousness.*

Bucke, an eminent psychiatrist, was 64 at the time, and had only a year to live. His early youth in Canada had been highly adventurous, and he had lost a foot and part of another whilst stranded in freezing temperatures in the Rockies after being attacked by Indians. An enthusiastic Socialist, he believed that the human race would soon enter a golden age, and that man would then evolve a higher kind of consciousness. A legacy enabled him to become a doctor, and at 39 he was appointed head of an insane asylum in Hamilton, Ontario. He moved to London, and in 1888 was elected President of the Psychological Section of the British Medical Association.

But the supreme experience that shaped his life had been a mystical illumination that had taken place in 1873. This is how he described it (speaking in the third person):

It was in the early spring at the beginning of his
thirty-sixth year. He and two friends had spent the
evening reading Wordsworth, Shelley, Keats,
Browning, and especially Whitman. They parted at
midnight, and he had a long drive in a hansom cab
… His mind, deeply under the influence of the
ideas, images and emotions called up by the reading
and talk of the evening, was calm and peaceful.
He was in a state of quiet, almost passive enjoyment.
All at once, without warning of any kind, he found
himself wrapped around as it were by a flame
colored cloud. For an instant he thought of fire,
some sudden conflagration in the great city, the next
he knew that the light was within himself. Directly
afterwards came upon him a sense of exultation, of
immense joyousness accompanied or immediately
followed by an intellectual illumination quite
impossible to describe. Into his brain streamed one
momentary lightning-flash of the Brahmic Splendor
which has ever since lightened his life; upon his
heart fell one drop of the Brahmic Bliss, leaving him
thenceforward for always an aftertaste of heaven.
Among other things he did not come to believe, he
saw and knew that the Cosmos is not dead matter
but a living Presence, that the soul of man is
immortal, that the universe is so built and ordered
that without any peradventure all things work
together for the good of each and all, that the

foundation principle of the world is what we call love and that the happiness of every one is in the long run absolutely certain. He claims that he learned more within the few seconds during which the illumination lasted than in previous months or even years of study, and that he learned much that no study could ever have taught.

The illumination itself continued not more than a few moments, but its effects proved ineffaceable; it was impossible for him ever to forget what he at that time saw and knew, neither did he, or could he, ever doubt the truth of what was then presented to his mind.

Bucke concluded that there is another form of consciousness, as far above self-consciousness as self-consciousness is above the ordinary consciousness of animals. His book *Cosmic Consciousness* is a study of dozens of examples from the Buddha to Whitman.

But Bucke couldn't actually define cosmic consciousness in any meaningful way. Let's see if we can do better.

William James quoted Bucke in his *Varieties of Religious Experience*. But James himself has an excellent essay called 'A Suggestion About Mysticism', which I quoted in my Foreword, and which goes to the heart of the matter. James suggests that mystical experience is not different *in kind* from ordinary consciousness, but is merely an extension of ordinary consciousness, and that even alcohol can produce a mild but valid mystical experience. He gives three of his own experiences, then goes on:

In each of the three like cases, the experience broke
in abruptly upon a perfectly commonplace situation
and lasted perhaps less than two minutes. In one
instance, I was engaged in conversation, but I doubt
whether my interlocutor noticed my abstraction.
What happened each time was that I seemed all at
once to be reminded of a past experience; and this
reminiscence, ere I could conceive or name it distinctly, developed into something further that
belonged with it, this in turn into something further
still, and so on, until the process faded out, leaving
me amazed at the sudden vision of increasing ranges
of distant facts of which I could give no articulate
account. The mode of consciousness was perceptual,
not conceptual – the field expanding so fast that
there seemed no time for conception or identifica-
tion to get in its work. There was a strongly exciting
sense that my knowledge of past (or present?) reality
was enlarging pulse by pulse, but so rapidly that my
intellectual processes could not keep up the pace.
The content was thus lost entirely to introspection –
it sank into the limbo into which dreams vanish
when we awake. The feeling – I won't call it belief –
that I had had a sudden opening, had seen through
a window, as it were, into distant realities that
incomprehensibly belonged with my own life, was
so acute that I cannot shake it off today.

Note also that he does not speak of seeing some distant 'mystical' realities, but of ranges of distant *fact*.

We could draw out the lesson of James's experience by saying that we think of 'consciousness' as a perception of individual things – that book, that teacup, etc. When we are bored, we seem to be *trapped* among objects (Sartre calls this 'nausea'). But James's comments offer a new insight: that consciousness is, by its very nature, *relational*, like a spider's web.

In 'normal consciousness', it is as if we are aware of ourselves in the centre of the web, and a few strands stretching around us, connecting us to objects. But when we are happy and excited – for example, setting out on holiday – our excitement seems to cause vibrations to spread down the web, and we get this feeling of connectedness with more distant realities. In moments of great illumination mystics feel that everything in the universe is connected to us by invisible threads.

Now since this book is as much about myself as about other people, let me add a personal anecdote. A few years ago I had spent the night at Dartington School after lecturing, but made the mistake of staying up too late discussing ideas, so that when I went to bed I didn't sleep a wink. Finally, at about 5am, I decided that I may as well sneak down to my car and drive home to Cornwall. But when I turned the key, the engine turned over very sluggishly, and went slower and slower, making me realize that a new battery I had recently purchased was a dud. I thought: Oh well, I'll just have to sneak back indoors, try and doze until eight o'clock, have breakfast, then persuade someone to drive me to the nearest garage to buy a battery ...

But first, I decided to sit there for a quarter of an hour, allowing the battery to get its breath back, then try again. To my relief, the engine started. A quarter of an hour later the sun came up. I found myself driving in a mood of intense happiness. I felt as Yeats felt in his London teashop: 'that I was blessèd and could bless'. And again, there was this strange sense of distant realities. But, unlike Yeats, I knew how it had come about. I had become intensely anxious to get the engine started, and had then been forced to discipline myself to sit still for a quarter of an hour, building a controlled mental discipline. This had the same effect as stretching a spring, and as soon as I was able to let go, it catapulted me into a state of 'intensity-consciousness', with a sense of being at the centre of the spider's web. It was a practical verification of James's 'suggestion about mysticism'.

In short, the whole experience, with its anxiety and tension, had caused me to raise my eyes above the narrow horizon of present experience. This is obviously a point of major importance. Why did Maslow's students keep on having PEs once they began discussing them with one another? Because discussing them made them raise their eyes beyond our usual worm's-eye view.

In *Cosmic Consciousness*, Bucke has a section on the Hindu saint and mystic Ramakrishna, and says that he is not sure whether he attained 'cosmic consciousness'. But since then, so much has been published on Ramakrishna that there can be no possible doubt about this.

I came upon Ramakrishna in a London public library in 1951, in a book called *Ramakrishna, Prophet of New India*, by Swami Nikhilananda, an abridgement of a larger work called

The Gospel of Sri Ramakrishna; I was instantly captivated by it.

He had been born into a Brahmin family in Bengal in 1836, and from an early age was absorbed by the mythology of Hinduism. His first mystical experience occurred when he was six or seven. He was then known as Gadadhar.

> At the age of six or seven Gadadhar had his first experience of spiritual ecstasy. One day in June or July, when he was walking along a narrow path between paddy-fields, eating the puffed rice that he carried in a basket, he looked up at the sky and saw a beautiful, dark thunder-cloud. As it spread, rapidly enveloping the whole sky, a flight of snow-white cranes passed in front of it. The beauty of the contrast overwhelmed the boy. He fell to the ground, unconscious, and the puffed rice went in all directions. Some villagers found him and carried him home in their arms. Gadadhar said later that in that state he had experienced an indescribable joy.

I recognized the experience immediately, although I had never experienced it with such intensity. As a child, Christmases had had this power to plunge me into a state of sheer happiness, in which it seemed obvious to me that *everything* is good. As a teenager, I could achieve the same state reading poets like Keats, Shelley and Whitman – like Bucke I regarded *Leaves of Grass* as among the greatest poetry ever written. So I could understand how the beauty of white cranes against a black storm cloud could induce ecstasy. I recognized this as the experience that G K Chesterton called 'absurd good news'.

So although my teens were an extremely difficult time, in which I was forced to work at jobs I hated – my working-class parents having insufficient money to send me to university – and there was even one occasion on which I seriously contemplated suicide, I never lost this basic feeling of optimism, the feeling that fate meant well by me, and indeed, by the whole human race.

This is why Ramakrishna came to occupy a central place in my first book *The Outsider*, written in my early twenties. The book begins with studies of pessimistic thinkers like Sartre, Camus, Hemingway, then continued with more 'positive' existentialists like Nietzsche, Tolstoy and Dostoevsky, and finally, religious figures like Van Gogh, George Fox, founder of Quakerism, William Blake, John Henry Newman and Ramakrishna. And since I had come close to suicide, I could understand the dark night of the soul that had caused Ramakrishna to despair:

> He felt the pangs of a child separated from its
> mother. Sometimes, in agony, he would rub his face
> against the ground and weep so bitterly that people,
> thinking he had lost his earthly mother, would
> sympathize with him in his grief. Sometimes, in
> moments of scepticism, he could cry: 'Art Thou
> true, Mother, or is it all fiction – mere poetry
> without any reality? If Thou dost exist, why do I not
> see Thee? Is religion a mere fantasy and art Thou
> only a figment of man's imagination?' Sometimes he

would sit on the prayer carpet for two hours like an inert object. He began to behave in an abnormal manner, most of the time unconscious of the world. He almost gave up food; and sleep left him altogether.

But he did not have to wait very long. He has thus described his first vision of the Mother: 'I felt as if my heart were being squeezed like a wet towel. I was overpowered with a great restlessness and a fear that it might not be my lot to realize Her in this life. I could not bear the separation from Her any longer. Life seemed to be not worth living. Suddenly my glance fell on the sword that was kept in the Mother's temple, I determined to put an end to my life. When I jumped up like a madman and seized it, suddenly the blessed Mother revealed Herself. The buildings with their different parts, the temple, and everything else vanished from my sight, leaving no trace whatsoever, and in their stead I saw a limitless, infinite, effulgent Ocean of Consciousness. As far as the eye could see, the shining billows were madly rushing at me from all sides with a terrific noise, to swallow me up! I was panting for breath. I was caught in the rush and collapsed, unconscious. What was happening in the outside world I did not know; but within me there was a steady flow of undiluted bliss, altogether new, and I felt the

presence of the Divine Mother.' On his lips when he
regained consciousness of the world was the word
'Mother'.

After this first experience of *samadhi* – divine bliss – Ramakishna
could thereafter be plunged into the same state by simply hearing
the name of Kali, the divine mother.

My own suicide attempt – by taking poison – had not ended
in any such blissful vision, but had left me overwhelmingly certain
that I did not want to die – on the contrary, I wanted *more* life.

It was also clear to me that Ramakrishna's *samadhi* was not the
answer, for it was, in a sense, a *passive* experience. It could not save
him from dying of cancer of the throat at the age of 50. What was
needed was something more like the affirmation of Nietzsche's
Zarathustra, with its explosion of ecstatic vitality.

What I learned from mystics and poets was that 'everyday consciousness' is only one of many possible states, and that we
become trapped in it by assuming that it is the only kind. But
Maslow's students discovered that all that was necessary to achieve
the states he called peak experiences was to talk about them and
think about them until you have reminded yourself how close they
are to our normal state.

Sometimes they seem to happen of their own accord, out of
the blue, as it were.

In 1969, the Oxford zoologist Sir Alister Hardy founded the
Religious Experience Research Unit at Oxford, to gather accounts
of religious experiences. A selection of these, published in *Seeing
the Invisible* (1990, edited by Meg Maxwell and Verena Tschudin)

reveals the extraordinary range of such experiences. The following may be regarded as typical:

> I was 16 and had always enjoyed solitary walks
> around my village home. One evening I set out, by
> myself, as usual, to walk up a lane towards the wood.
> I was not feeling particularly happy or particularly
> sad, just ordinary. I was certainly not 'looking' for
> anything, just going for a walk to be peaceful. It
> must have been August, because the corn was ripe
> and I only had a summer dress and sandals on. I was
> almost to the wood when I paused, turned to look at
> the cornfield, took two or three steps forward so I
> was able to touch the ears of corn and watched them
> swaying in the faint breeze. I looked to the end of
> the field – it had a hedge then – and beyond that to
> some tall trees towards the village. The sun was over
> to my left; it was not in my eyes.
>
> Then … there must be a blank. I will never know
> for how long, because I was only in my normal
> conscious mind with normal faculties as I came out
> of it. Everywhere surrounding me was this white,
> bright, sparkling light, like sun on frosty snow, like a
> million diamonds, and there was no cornfield, no
> trees, no sky, this light was everywhere; my ordinary
> eyes were open, but I was not seeing with them. It
> can only have lasted a moment I think or I would
> have fallen over.

The feeling was indescribable, but I have never experienced anything in the years that followed that can compare with that glorious moment; it was blissful, uplifting, I felt open-mouthed wonder.

Then the tops of the trees became visible once again, then a piece of sky and gradually the light was no more, and the cornfield was spread before me. I stood there for a long time, trying in vain for it to come back and have tried many times since, but I only saw it once; but I know in my heart it is still there – and here – and everywhere around us. I know Heaven is within us and around us. I have had this wonderful experience which brought happiness beyond compare.

The most significant phrase here is: 'I know in my heart it is still there'. Her vision has gone back to normal, but she is aware that, with some slight adjustment, it could once again show her the world illuminated by 'absurd good news'.

Her experience has much in common with Ramakrishna's vision of white birds against a storm cloud. In this case, what triggered it seems to be reaching out to touch the swaying ear of corn.

The sense of time standing still often seems to occur in these mystical experiences, as in this one that follows immediately on the previous experience:

I was relaxed and happy as I walked. Suddenly, everything stopped. I stopped. The birds were no

longer singing. The distant traffic sounds from the
village ceased. Nothing moved. Utter silence, utter
stillness. The May sunlight was transformed into a
white radiance.

I don't know how long the experience lasted.
The light softened into an afternoon glow. Once
more the breeze rustled the leaves, the birds sang
and I could hear a faraway car. I walked on.

The vision transformed me. I stepped from it
into a transfigured world; from agnosticism to
gnosis. Everything connected.

Many such experiences are accompanied by a strong feeling of
love and benevolence. In the following case, a woman who had
been on holiday had left her spare key with a crotchety, talkative
old neighbour. When he failed to appear the next morning she
experienced a momentary fear that there was something wrong,
perhaps that he was dead.

I said casually to my husband, 'You'd better look in
to see how old C is.' A few minutes later I heard
them chatting and laughing in the street outside.
'Good, he's all right then,' I thought with relief. As I
said these words to myself, the kitchen and garden
were filled with golden light. I became conscious
that at the centre of the Universe, and in my garden,
was a great pulsing dynamo that ceaselessly poured
out love. This love poured over and through me,

and I was part of it and it wholly encompassed me.
Perfectly me, I was perfectly part of perfection.

The vision was gone in a moment, leaving me
with a strong desire to rush out and embrace anyone
I could find, including Mr C! At the same time, I
had a very strong feeling that the vision was holy
and not to be chatted about. Indeed, I did not speak
of it except to my husband for some years. Another
apprehension was that it was outside time. I also
find the words I use to describe it quite inadequate.
It was overwhelmingly real, more real than anything
I had experienced, although I had been in love, and
the feelings after the birth of each of my children
had been wonderful. The vision was of a far 'realer'
quality. To deny it would be the ultimate sin,
blasphemy.

Here she clearly believes that it was her sudden concern for
another person that triggered the experience of universal love, as
if some benevolent entity had rewarded her.

In a case that I personally find the most interesting, a radio
operator who had fought in a tank battle in the Western Desert in
the Second World War was relaxing under the stars in a state of
exhaustion, thinking about the meaning of his life.

The dust of battle, which had obscured the sky, had
quite gone, and the stars were enormous and
magnificent. A slight breeze came from the warm

sea nearby and the air seemed to be slightly perfumed, from what source I could not imagine.

Suddenly – and it really was quite sudden – my train of thought accelerated and vastly improved in quality (I am trying to choose my words carefully to describe what happened). New and convincing ideas came into my mind in a steady torrent, flaws in my existing ideas were illuminated and as I made mental corrections to them the diminishing gaps in the logical sequence were filled by neat, brand-new linking concepts which made a beautiful logical pattern.

I was immediately aware that this was important to me as nothing had been before. The impact was so powerful that for a split second I felt something akin to fear, but this I rejected quickly because, simultaneously, I was enjoying an almost, nay actually, physical thrill of delight. Yes, I think delight is the right word.

What I want to stress most (and this taxes my powers of description) is that a small, everyday, critical part of my brain was standing apart, observing with astonishment what was going on in the rest of my thinking apparatus. How long the experience lasted I hesitate to estimate, but it was probably not more than ten minutes – perhaps less.

After only a few seconds 'I' realized that no effort of mine was involved in what, for me, was a highly

superior piece of thinking and, moreover, it was
taking place with an energetic authority which was
unlike anything I had ever known about myself
(I was always a cautious, doubtful thinker). That
small watch-dog part of my brain marvelled at this
as it happened. This ability to experience thought on
two quite distinct levels simultaneously is something
I have never heard mentioned as being possible, and
I feel inadequate to describe it! It has never recurred.

There was no specific 'religious' aspect in the
pattern of ideas which presented itself to me. It had
to do with man's (my) position in relation to the
universe; it dealt with eternity, which became readily
understandable; with infinity, which faced one with
ultimate fear unless the next stage in the logic was
appreciated – strangely enough (as I thought then)
to do with the relationship between the sexes. And
so on, until, as suddenly as it had started, the train
of thought paused, at a very reasonable point, and
added, as a definite statement, 'That's quite enough
to be going on with.'

I remember taking a deep breath and exclaiming
aloud 'You can say that again!'

He goes on to add: 'The point I must make is this: I find it
impossible to believe that what happened originated inside me.
Perhaps, unwittingly, I tapped some universal source of
knowledge.'

Perhaps the most important single discussion of 'cosmic consciousness' ever written is a chapter in P D Ouspensky's *New
Model of the Universe* called 'Experimental Mysticism'. Ouspensky
does not reveal the way he achieved his states of 'higher consciousness', but I suspect it was simply through nitrous oxide, which
William James had also used.

Ouspensky describes how, as soon as he went into a higher
level of consciousness, he found it quite impossible to say anything
about it because saying anything would require saying everything
– because everything is connected together: 'everything is
explained by something else and in turn explains another thing.
There is nothing separate ... In order to describe the first impressions, the first sensations, it is necessary to describe all at once. The
new world with which one comes into contact has no sides, so that
it is impossible to describe first one side and then the other. All of
it is visible at every point ...' i.e. bird's-eye consciousness.

Another significant observation is that time seemed to slow
down. He began a sentence with the words 'I said yesterday', and
the word 'I' aroused a thousand ideas about the mystery of indi-
viduality; the word 'said' aroused a thousand ideas about the
mystery of communication; the word 'yesterday' aroused a
thousand thoughts about time. And by that time, he had forgotten
what he was going to say anyway.

Looking at an ashtray, Ouspensky felt that it was a kind of key
to the universe, and he tried to write down on paper what he was
'seeing'. Later, he discovered he had written a single sentence: 'One
could go mad from one ashtray.'

In his poem 'Under Ben Bulben', written towards the end of his life, Yeats talks about how, 'when a man is fighting mad':

> Something drops from eyes long blind,
> *He completes his partial mind*,
> For an instant stands at ease
> Laughs aloud, his heart at peace.
> (My italics)

This is not unlike Dostoevsky's experience when he was reprieved from the firing squad. But it is so important because it recognizes that ordinary consciousness is somehow *incomplete*, like the moon in its last quarter. You know the whole moon is really there, yet you can stare as hard as you like and you still can't see it. In these moments of illumination, the whole moon suddenly becomes visible: the 'partial mind' momentarily becomes the whole mind, and we feel god-like. It is vitally important to realize that 'ordinary consciousness' is incomplete. In fact, to put it more emphatically, *everyday consciousness is a liar*.

As a schoolboy, Robert Graves also experienced something of the sort, and he describes it in a story called 'The Abominable Mr Gunn'. He describes how, sitting on the roller behind the cricket pavilion, he quite suddenly 'knew everything'. He says that he didn't literally 'know everything' (i.e. the date of the battle of Borodino), but that this was a point of view that *made sense of everything* – what we have been calling a bird's-eye view. It was still there when he woke up the next morning, but when he tried to write it down, he began to correct and cross out, and it gradually faded, giving way to 'the light of common day'.

But Graves adds an important gloss to this experience. He speaks of a boy in the class called Smilley who could instantaneously see the answer to complex mathematical problems. The mathematics master, Mr Gunn, hated this and caned him until he behaved more 'normally'.

Now in fact, many such people exist, including two mentally deficient twins, known as idiots savants, in a New York hospital. They can go on quoting huge prime numbers at one another for hours. A prime is a number that cannot be divided exactly by any smaller number. Examples of prime numbers are 3, 5 and 7; 9 isn't because it can be divided by 3. But there is no way of working out whether some huge number is a prime, except by painfully and slowly dividing every smaller number into it. Yet these twins – like hundreds of other calculating prodigies – can sit there quoting 20-digit primes at one another. In some odd way, they are hovering over the whole number field, like a bird, and doing something that is, mathematically speaking, impossible.

There is a part of our mind which *knows* things that the ordinary conscious self does not know. I have experienced this many times. In the 1960s, returning from Scotland and prepared for a very long drive to the Scottish border, I suddenly realized that it was far closer than I had imagined – by 50 miles – and that by mid-afternoon I could probably reach the house of an old friend in Leeds. This so filled me with pleasure and optimism that I again went into a kind of mini-cosmic consciousness as I drove along, my mind bubbling with exhilaration. Fifty miles or so further on, as I drove through the Lake District, I could not only *see* the vast hills on either side of the road, but in some odd way I could *sense* the hills that lay beyond them, as if part of my mind was a quarter of a mile up above the car. The sceptical commentator will say, 'Pure delusion', or at least, mere 'feeling.' Yet I had a very clear sense that it was far more than this: that in some odd way, it was as if a spider's web was stretching around me in all directions, and that by focusing on any given 'strand', vibrations could travel down the strand to provide me with objective information.

Yet such 'glimpses' only raise again in my mind the question of why they are so difficult to recreate. Ouspensky describes the dreariness of returning to 'everyday consciousness' after his mystical experiments. These, he says, usually ended in sleep, and his awakening the next morning was always a depressing and disappointing experience. The ordinary world seemed unutterably dull:

> … this world contained something extraordinarily oppressive: it was incredibly empty, colourless and lifeless. It was as though everything in it was wooden, as if it was an enormous wooden machine with creaking wooden wheels, wooden thoughts, wooden moods, wooden sensations; everything was terribly slow, scarcely moved, or moved with a melancholy wooden creaking. Everything was dead, soulless, feelingless.
>
> They were terrible, these moments of awakening in an unreal world after a real one, in a dead world after a living, in a limited world, cut into small pieces, after an infinite and entire world.

Rudolf Steiner once said, 'Never complain about your lot in life – you chose it before you were born'. Which only raises the question: why would anyone choose this 'wooden world' with its creaking mill-wheels?

Where Ouspensky was concerned it is not difficult to answer that question. He was a typical Russian romantic, and what Nietzsche would have called a 'world-rejector'. He had a streak of self-pity that led him to end his days as a hopeless alcoholic. It is the same romanticism that made the early Yeats dream of escaping to fairyland. But Yeats differs from most of that 'tragic generation' of the 1890s in that he succeeded in outgrowing it, and turning into the realist who wrote 'Under Ben Bulben'.

This is the answer to the question of Ouspensky's 'wooden world'. It is also the answer that Nietzsche recognized instinctively as the answer to the problem of romanticism that wreaked so much havoc in the 19th century, and that Shaw was talking about when he said: 'Every dream can be willed into reality by those who are strong enough to believe in it.'

Chapter Five

The Near and the Far

In 1905 the Czech composer Vitezslav Novak wrote a tone poem called 'Of the Eternal Longing'. Based on a story by Hans Andersen, it is intended a symbolize his own sense of loneliness. A swan migrating with her flock to warmer climes falls from the sky with exhaustion, and floats all night on the sea. But as the dawn rises, she recovers her strength and flies on alone. The beautiful, sad music evokes the 'eternal longing' of the title, the composer's own sense of isolation.

My own Czech recording of the piece has a cover painting as beautiful as the title, showing a view over a mediaeval city square on a starlit night, with pointed rooftops and towers. The jester Till Eulenspiegel, whose tone poem by Strauss shares the record, sits with his feet dangling over the parapet of a high tower. This picture seems to me to capture the essence of the eternal longing, which can be expressed in music so much more effectively than in words.

Now it so happens that we can give an exact date for the birth of musical romanticism, more than two centuries ago.

It was in the summer of 1793 when two young men set out on

a tour of southern Germany. They were a strangely contrasted pair: one physically robust and full of vitality, the other slender, pale and effeminate. The stronger of the two, although only 20, had already begun to acquire himself a reputation as a writer, and would eventually become one of the most influential storytellers of his generation; his friend – who has been described as a 'girlish, helpless creature' – was a musician and a dreamer. Their names – which have been virtually forgotten in our own age – were Ludwig Tieck and Wilhelm Wackenroder. That tour of ancient cities – like Bamberg and Nuremberg – was to have a tremendous impact on these two young men, and, through them, on the rest of Europe.

Tieck, the son of a Berlin ropemaker, had been a friend of Wackenroder since childhood. Strictly speaking, Wackenroder was socially his superior, since his father was a senior civil servant. As far as Wackenroder was concerned, this was a misfortune, for his father was determined that the son should become a success in life; young Wilhelm regarded the very idea of 'success' as revolting. He was shy and melancholy, happy only when listening to music. His friend Tieck was altogether less sensitive to music; his taste was for stronger meat – tales of blood and horror, with a strong infusion of the supernatural. Nevertheless, the two adored one another with an abandonment that would nowadays lead to an assumption of homosexuality, but which was, in fact, almost certainly innocent.

Franconia is the home of the excellent *steinwein*, sold in flat circular bottles, and no doubt the friends drank their share of it in that summer of 1793. I can well understand the impact on the two young men, for I experienced it myself in the summer of 1957, a year after the publication of *The Outsider*. Driving down the Rhine, with its ancient towns, was like being transported back five centuries.

For Tieck and Wackenroder, what made that trip memorable was not just the wine, but visits to old churches and mediaeval towns, many of them still looking much as they had in the days of the minnesingers of the Middle Ages. For Wackenroder, all this came as a revelation; the Berliner fell in love with the romantic charm of southern Germany, and was overwhelmed by the magnificence of mediaeval art. When he returned to Berlin in the following year, and was forced to enter the Prussian civil service by his father (who was to become Minister of Justice), he spent many tearful hours daydreaming of ancient cobbled streets, gabled houses and Gothic cathedrals. In due course, he and Tieck consoled themselves by collaborating on a book called *Heartpourings of an Art-loving Monk (Herzensergiessungen eines kunstliebenden Klosterbruders)*, which was published anonymously – no doubt to prevent their fathers from finding out what they had been doing – in 1797. The sickly Wackenroder had only one more year to live; bored and depressed by the life of a civil servant, he died of typhoid at the age of 25. Tieck was plunged into grief. In the following year, he published Wackenroder's posthumous papers – with contributions by himself – under the title *Fantasies on Art*.

The impact of the *Heartpourings of an Art-loving Monk* – with its essays on Dürer, Michelangelo, Leonardo and Raphael – was tremendous; it became the bible of a generation, the most influential book since Goethe's *Sorrows of Young Werther* two decades earlier.

Its most influential chapter was a story called 'The Remarkable Life of the Musician Joseph Berglinger'. Berglinger, says the art-loving monk, was a friend of his youth. His mother died giving birth to him, leaving the father, a poverty-stricken doctor, to bring up a family of six. They grew like 'weeds in a neglected garden'. But the young Joseph, 'whose whole life was a beautiful fantasy and a heavenly dream', was obsessed by music. When he went to church to hear sacred oratorios, he stood there amidst the crowd, 'his brain paralysed with empty earthly trivialities'. But as soon as the organ sounded, 'long drawn and mighty as a wind from heaven', 'it seemed to him as though his soul had unfurled great wings; he felt himself raised up above the barren heath ... and he soared into the radiant sky.' To us the image sounds commonplace enough; to Wackenroder's young contemporaries it was new and strange and unutterably exciting. 'The present sank away before him; his soul was cleansed of all the pettiness of this world – mere dust on the soul's lustre; the music set his nerves tingling with a gentle thrill, calling up changing images before him with every change in the music.' 'At certain passages, an isolated beam of light fell on his soul; at this, it seemed to him as though he all at once grew wiser and was looking down, with clearer sight and a certain inspired and placid melancholy, on all the busy world below.' (Wagner was later to speak of 'art that makes life appear like a game, and withdraws us from the common fate'.) But then comes the problem that was to torment all the great Romantics: that the moment Berglinger walks out into the street, 'the rapture vanished like a gleaming cloud'.

'His whole life long he was tormented by this bitter dissension between his inborn lofty enthusiasm and our common mortal lot, which breaks in daily on our reveries, forcibly bringing us down to earth.'

And so it goes on, for page after page, describing the ecstasies that Berglinger experiences through music, and the intense misery of being forced to return to the trivialities of everyday life.

Finally, Berglinger decides to follow his 'inner voice', and runs away from home to make his way to the nearest great city. There he eventually becomes Kapellmeister in the palace of a prince of the Church.

But it is a disappointing life. He performs great works of art, even performs his own symphonies; yet he feels that these German philistines fail to understand him. Instead of fellow spirits ennobled by great music, he finds only spite and envy. 'In my youth I thought to avoid the misery of earthy life; now, more than ever, I have sunk into the mire.' Then he is called to his father's deathbed, and is appalled to see the poverty in which his sisters are living. From then on, 'his tortured heart would not let him recover himself'. In one final tremendous effort, he composes a great oratorio in which he expresses all his sufferings and all his ecstasies. 'His soul was like that of the invalid who, in a strange paroxysm, exhibits greater strength than the healthy man.' The performance of his oratorio on Easter Sunday leaves him weak and exhausted, and he dies soon after. 'Oh why,' asks the art-loving monk, 'did heaven ordain that the struggle between lofty enthusiasm and the common misery of this earth make him unhappy all his life, and in the end tear apart the twofold nature of his mind and body?'

This story, scarcely a dozen pages long, would become perhaps the most influential work on music ever written.

It was sad that Wackenroder had to die to inspire a generation, but that is more or less the truth of it. For as a dead writer, he passed into legend in a way that is impossible for the living.

It was in 1797, the year before Wackenroder's death, that Tieck made the acquaintance of another brilliant young writer, Friedrich von Schlegel, who was intended for a career in banking before he persuaded his parents to allow him to go to the University at Göttingen. Fascinated by the ancient Greeks, he had already done for them what Wackenroder did for the Italian Renaissance, holding them up as an ideal society where artists and poets can feel at home. Tieck and Schlegel were impressed by one another – Tieck was already famous as the author of some remarkable melodramatic novels and ghost stories – and when Schlegel moved to the University of Jena, to join his elder brother August, Tieck was also inspired to move there.

Jena and its sister-town Weimar were Germany's cultural centres. That was largely because, in 1775, when Wackenroder and Tieck were only two years old, Goethe had moved to Weimar. Two years earlier, he had published *The Sorrows of Young Werther*, a novel that made all Europe weep and caused an epidemic of suicides. Duke Karl August, who had brought Goethe to Weimar, was delighted to find that the 26-year-old poet was a man of practical judgement, and appointed him Privy Councillor. Weimar soon became the literary capital of Germany (or of the conglomeration of states that later became Germany). Twelve years later, Goethe was joined by the brilliant and rebellious poet Friedrich

Schiller, an ex-army surgeon whose play *The Robbers* (1780) had caused as great a sensation as *Young Werther*. Oddly enough, Goethe and Schiller were at first hostile to one another, and Goethe found Schiller a job as a professor of history at nearby Jena simply to get him out of Weimar.

In 1794, the year after Tieck and Wackenroder had made their momentous tour of Franconia, Goethe and Schiller met at a session of the Natural History Society in Jena, and quickly became close friends. Schiller had recently signed a contract to edit a literary magazine called *Die Horen* (Horae, in Greek mythology, were the goddesses of the seasons). He asked a gifted young literary critic, August Wilhelm von Schlegel, to come and help him edit it, and in due course Schlegel's younger brother Friedrich joined him. Now Friedrich became the chief theoretician of the new 'Romantic' movement – he virtually invented the word – and the house he shared with his brother became the meeting place of like-minded enthusiasts. The poet Novalis, one of the most extreme and gifted of the Romantics, joined them in Jena in 1799. And in the same year, Tieck also moved to Jena.

The most famous of his novels, *Blond Eckbert* (written before Wackenroder's death), is a preposterous but oddly moving piece of nonsense about a man who accidentally marries his own sister and ends by going mad; its basic message seems to be that life is a dream or a cruel hoax. And in 1798, Tieck published an unfinished novel which he had planned with Wackenroder, *Franz Sternbald's Wanderings*, about a young painter, a pupil of Dürer, who wanders off to Italy in search of his true identity. This is an odd mixture of Wackenroder's idealization of the Middle Ages – the 'age of faith and art' – and Tieck's favourite scenery – mountains, crags, impenetrable forests and ruined castles. The hero is initiated into the delights of love, and this, in turn, is nourished by music, 'the most heavenly of all the arts'. 'If one is to believe in purgatory, where the soul is purified and chastened by pain, so, on the contrary, music is a pre-heaven, in which this purification is effected by melancholy bliss.' And when the hero encounters a beautiful girl he has seen in childhood visions, and sinks to his knees in front of her, a horn proceeds to 'improvise with the most thrilling tones' – an anticipation of cinematographic musical scores – until he is not sure whether he is awake or dreaming.

All this explains why Tieck was received with open arms by the Jena Romantics, and why his friend's tale of the musician Joseph Berglinger became the book they loved most.

Now it so happened that another influential new recruit had also joined the Schlegels in Jena: Friedrich von Schelling, the author of a remarkable work called *Ideas Towards a Philosophy of Nature* (1797). In 1798, he was appointed to the chair of philosophy in the university. And at the time when Wackenroder's ideas on music were filling the Romantics with a delicious sense of melancholy, Schelling's writings on nature were conjuring up equally moving visions of distant hills and far horizons, and of a great spiritual force that conceals itself behind the face of material reality.

As strange as it sounds to modern ears, few people in the 18th century regarded nature as beautiful. In fact, most people looked upon mountains and forests as rather sinister. Even Tieck, that arch-priest of Romanticism, uses them as mere stage scenery against which to set his hair-raising melodramas.

Schelling's *Philosophy of Nature* changed all that – along with an extraordinary novel called *Hesperus* by an eccentric humorist named Jean Paul Richter who became famous all over Europe under the name Jean Paul. A clergyman's son who had spent his childhood and youth in extreme poverty, and even as a student at Leipzig came close to starvation, Richter was past 30 when *Hesperus* burst upon the world and turned him into a cult figure who was worshipped by the new generation.

Anyone who is tempted to borrow a copy of *Hesperus* from the library to see what all the fuss was about will be sorely puzzled. For this thousand-page monster was influenced by Laurence Sterne's comic masterpiece *Tristram Shandy,* and at least half its length is taken up with rambling digressions on anything that takes the author's fancy. What made it so popular was its highly romantic plot about two close friends who are in love with the same girl – who finally turns out to be the sister of one of them.

Victor and Flamin have been educated together in England, and regard one another with a romantic passion that would nowadays lead to the suspicion that they are gay. (However, in the late 18th century, close male friends were always flinging their arms round one another and bursting into tears.) When the handsome Victor returns from another stint of education at medical school, Flamin takes him to the top of an ivy-clad tower (another staple of Romanticism) and confesses that he is in love with a beautiful girl called Clotilde, the daughter of the local prince, and is terrified that she will prefer Victor. Victor tenderly assures him that nothing is less likely. But when Victor meets Clotilde at a garden party, he is instantly smitten. And the girl seems to feel the same. What is to be done?

Later that evening, Victor's father, Lord Horion, reveals a strange secret. Flamin is actually the son of the prince, and therefore Clotilde's brother. Clotilde already knows this, and has been sworn to silence. The explanation of the deception is that Horion, an Englishman who is the prince's chief minister, had been afraid that Flamin would become as corrupt as his libertine father, and had spirited him away with Victor to be educated in England. And now Flamin wants to marry his own sister, it is a somewhat delicate situation.

Then Victor and Clotilde meet by chance in the woods and confess their love. Flamin, who finds them in one another's arms, assumes he has been betrayed and tries to kill Victor. He fails, but Victor feels obliged to renounce his love and go travelling in Europe. Flamin, tormented by guilt, becomes a recluse. Finally he learns the truth, and is contemplating suicide by flinging himself from the ivy-covered tower when he hears a sound, and turns to find Clotilde and Victor behind him. Both put an arm round his waist and lead him back home, and so all ends more or less happily.

The modern reader would find it hard to imagine how this preposterous concoction achieved such popularity. So did I – until I actually tried reading it, and found it all so oddly moving and exciting, and I could see exactly why it swept across Europe just as Richardson's *Pamela* had in 1740. It is full of exquisite little scenes of natural beauty, and together with Schelling's *Philosophy of Nature*, created a passion for woods, mountains and moonlit ruins.

For the impecunious Jean Paul its success represented salvation. It came at just the right time, when failure to find a publisher had led him to return home to live with his mother, who had only a widow's pension. He was 32 when *Hesperus* made him famous. From then until his death 30 years later (1825) he was one of Germany's best-loved writers, and novels like *Titan* (on which Mahler based a symphony) may be said to have taught Europe to surrender to 'the eternal longing'.

But even by the time of Jean Paul's death, Romanticism was encountering a predictable problem. Dreams of starry nights and quaint mediaeval towns were all very well, but what happened when you woke up the next morning and had to go to work? The dreams made it twice as hard to put up with everyday trivialities. Many would-be poets whose fathers wanted them to go into commerce must have felt that Wackenroder was well out of it.

Novalis, a young aristocrat whose real name was Friedrich von Hardenberg, became engaged to a beautiful 14-year-old girl, and lost the will to live when she died of a liver complaint. That, and his brother's death shortly thereafter, had the effect of turning him into a religious mystic, whose work would have an immense effect on the young generation. His *Hymns to the Night* are the classic expression of the poet's longing to return to the darkness. The hero of his unfinished novel *Heinrich von Ofterdingen* spends his life in a vain search for a blue flower that he has glimpsed in a vision. Novalis would die at the age of 29.

In England the spirit of Romanticism made one of its earliest appearances in the person of William Blake, also a poet and mystic. Born in 1757, Blake published *The Marriage of Heaven and*

Hell in 1793, when Jean Paul was writing *Hesperus*. Blake's parents were members of a congregation in Fetter Lane, London, presided over by a strange German mystic called Count Ludwig von Zinzendorf, whose religious teachings were held in high esteem by the parents of Novalis. It was not until 2003 that the American scholar Martha Schuchard revealed just how peculiar were the doctrines of the mystical count. In *Why Mrs Blake Cried: The Sexual Basis of Spiritual Vision*, we learn that Zinzendorf went through a spiritual crisis that culminated in the realization that there is a close connection between religious ecstasy and sexual ecstasy. Members of this Jesus-oriented congregation, like Blake's father and mother, were initiated into sexual ceremonies which induced a mystical/sexual state that often lasted all night. In effect, they were practising a kind of sexual yoga. The mystic Emanuel Swedenborg, another member of the sect, had arrived independently at the same conclusions about the connection between religion and sex.

Blake was still a baby when his parents ceased to be members of the congregation, so there can have been no direct influence. But Zinzendorf was convinced that children can be taught even in the womb, and it is tempting to speculate that Zinzendorf's sexual doctrines – and the sexual yoga of Mr and Mrs Blake – influenced him before he was born, and explains the powerful sexual teaching of works like *Visions of the Daughters of Albion*. The reason 'Mrs Blake cried' was not simply because her husband proposed going to bed with the maid, but because he held views about the delights of promiscuity that must certainly have shocked her. It would be another century and a half before such views were promulgated by the liberated hippies of the 1960s.

Even by the time of Blake's death at the age of 70 in 1827, the doctrines of sexual freedom had come to play a central part in Romanticism. Driven out of England in 1814 by Anglo-Saxon puritanism, Byron and Shelley became symbols of sexual dissipation, and spent the remainder of their lives abroad. Byron, the embodiment of romantic rebellion, became the most celebrated poet in Europe and America. (He noted that in spite of his popularity in England, his sales in France, Germany and America were even larger.)

Yet when Byron died in 1824, fighting with the Greeks against the Turks, Romanticism virtually died with him. It was the same in Germany after the death of Jean Paul in the following year. His work lost its popularity almost immediately. And the death of Goethe in 1832, at the age of 83, might be regarded as the full stop that brought the epoch of blissful heart-pourings to an end.

This was not, of course, because the 'eternal longing' suddenly evaporated. On the contrary, it remained more powerful than ever. What had evaporated was the optimism that had bubbled out of *Hesperus*, and that had made Wordsworth write of the French Revolution: 'Bliss was it in that dawn to be alive'. It was the collapse of belief in the power of the human spirit to conquer, to achieve new levels of freedom. The pessimism that was already inherent in *Young Werther* and *The Robbers* and *Hymns to the Night* had become the spirit of the age. The Industrial Revolution only made things worse, for it made the poets and artists feel that if this was what conquest was all about, then they preferred defeat. The *liebestod* of *Tristan and Isolde* was a rejection of everything the 19th century stood for.

So the end of the century, the 1890s saw the Romantic quest end in gloom and defeat. Yeats called them 'the tragic generation', all those poets and artists who died of drink or dissipation or discouragement: Lionel Johnson, Francis Thompson, Aubrey Beardsley, Oscar Wilde, James Thomson, Ernest Dowson, Paul Verlaine, Arthur Rimbaud. Yeats's alcoholic friend Dowson symbolizes the spirit of the nineties in all its elegiac sadness with his poem 'Dregs', which is quoted in chapter one.

The poets of Yeats's 'tragic generation' certainly believed in those glimpses of bliss that illuminate the human spirit, and bring a sense of freedom; but they felt we have no control over them. The spirit of man is like an oxy-acetylene flame that can burn underwater. But sooner or later, the water will close in and extinguish it.

What destroyed Romanticism, as much as anything, was a sense of increasing realism. Those early Romantics, like Rousseau and the young Goethe and Schiller and Jean Paul, felt that freedom was just around the corner. After the death of Byron, this seemed to be an illusion. Yeats summarized it all in a sad little poem entitled 'The Wheel':

> Through winter-time we call on spring,
> And through the spring on summer call,
> And when the abounding hedges ring
> Declare that winter's best of all;
> And after that there's nothing good
> Because the spring-time has not come –

Nor know that what disturbs our blood
Is but its longing for the tomb.

The longing for freedom is seen as a futile craving for change, the view Schopenhauer had expressed in his nihilistic *World as Will and Illusion*.

In the 20th century, this mood of sadness and defeat turned into something more like gloomy stoicism. In Villiers de Lisle-Adam's *Axel*, the hero says contemptuously: 'As for living, our servants can do that for us.' He is declaring that 'real life' is too crude and stupid to be worth the effort. In *Ulysses*, James Joyce seems to have accepted the world's brutal materialism and crude reality – E M Forster described it as 'a determined attempt to cover the universe in mud' – yet this is really disappointed Romanticism. The surrealistic Night Town scene is full of a kind of violent rage, as if he is shaking his fist at the world of matter – like Dylan Thomas raging against the dying of the light.

The dilemma is expressed with unusual clarity in L H Myers' 1935 novel *The Near and the Far*. In the opening chapter, the young Prince Jali looks out from the battlements of a castle in the capital of Akbar the Great; he and his family have travelled there for a great conference. As he looks over the desert towards the magnificent sunset, Jali reflects that there are *two* deserts, one of which is a glory to the eye, and the other of which is a weariness to the foot. And there is no way of bringing these two together. If he now rushed downstairs and ran towards the sunset, he would merely get his shoes full of sand. The 'near and the far' remain irreconcilable. Or, as Yeats put it in 'Towards Break of Day':

Nothing that we love over-much
Is ponderable to our touch.

As previously discussed, a kind of grim stoicism took hold in the first half of the 20th century after the sad defeatism of the 1890s. This new philosophy called itself Existentialism, a term that had been invented in the mid-19th century by the Dane Søren Kierkegaard as a criticism of German philosophy, particularly Hegel. Kierkegaard complained that what ordinary people need is not some gaseous, idealistic philosophy about history and the universe, but an answer to the question of what we ought to do with our lives. Its basic question is: what am I doing here? As a Christian, Kierkegaard felt that the answer was: searching for salvation. But a century later, a new generation of existentialists like Jaspers, Heidegger, Sartre and Camus declined religious consolations and insisted that man must learn to stand on his own feet. And in the Introduction to a collection of existentialist texts, *The Search for Being* (1962), Walter Kimmel uses the phrase 'the fundamental alienation of beings from the source of power, meaning and purpose', which is perhaps the best encapsulation of the problem that has been achieved. In short, the aim – the basic human aim – is to regain contact with 'the source of power, meaning and purpose' – what I have labelled 'power consciousness.'

In his early book, *The Myth of Sisyphus*, Camus says that Sisyphus, as a punishment from the gods, has to keep on rolling a rock uphill, and watch it roll down again for ever – yet, he says, we must imagine Sisyphus happy, because in spite of physical servitude, he still possesses *internal freedom*. And here we can immediately see the connection between Romanticism and Existentialism. Byron, in the 'The Prisoner of Chillon', had written:

> Eternal spirit of the chainless mind
> Brightest in dungeons, liberty thou art!

This makes us aware that Existentialism is simply, you might say, 'Romanticism Mark 2', and that its starting point is a recognition of the reality of human freedom – for example, Sartre made the interesting comment that he had never felt so free as when he was in the French Resistance, and was likely to be arrested and shot at any moment. But it also takes it for granted that human life is totally meaningless. Hemingway summarized his own version of this 'existential stoicism' when he wrote 'A man can be destroyed but not defeated.'

But what if – like myself – we have a powerful bias in favour of being neither destroyed *nor* defeated?

Philosophically speaking, I have devoted all my writing life to trying to create what might be called 'Romanticism Mark 3' – a positive existentialism, that declines to accept this 'premise of meaninglessness' that is found in Sartre, Camus, Foucault, Derrida and other fashionable thinkers of the past 50 years. This 'new existentialism', based upon the phenomenological method of Edmund Husserl, is the intellectual foundation of my own 'non-pessimistic existentialism'.

Before the end of this book, I will ask the reader to take a deep breath and plunge with me into the history of modern philosophy, to grasp precisely what went wrong.

Chapter Six

The Paradoxes
of Nihilism

In November 1958, Samuel Beckett's play *Endgame* came to the
Royal Court Theatre in London. I was at the first night, and
disliked it intensely for, unlike *Waiting for Godot*, it seemed to me
so unutterably dreary and negative that I was surprised that the
audience did not walk out. It differed from *Godot* in that it was not
even remotely entertaining. But then, I had already sat through the
French version *Fin de Partie* a year earlier. Following that occasion,
the theatre critic Kenneth Tynan had had some harsh words to say,
accusing Beckett of seeing man 'as a pygmy who connives at his own
degradation'. I waited with interest to see what he would have to say
in *The Observer* the following Sunday about this English version,
which had been preceded by an even gloomier playlet called
Krapp's Last Tape, in which a man records a kind of last will and
testament into a tape recorder.

To my surprise, there was no review – only a parody entitled 'Slamm's
Last Knock', in which a cripple in a wheelchair talks about the futility of life, while his parents sit on either side of him in dustbins.

What seemed clear was that Tynan was hedging his bets. He hated the play, but since the previous year, had watched Beckett's intellectual star rising steadily among the literati, and was now not quite so willing to parade his reservations. So parody was a good excuse for saying nothing.

I was not unsympathetic, because it was obvious that Tynan did not even know where to begin to attack Beckett's pessimism. Being faced with nihilism is rather like finding your path blocked by a large chunk of concrete. Unless you can get your crowbar *underneath* it, it is virtually immovable.

This is the problem with nihilism. It is hard to get underneath it. We attempt to refute most doubtful propositions by trying to demonstrate their lack of logic, but the assertion: 'Everything is self-evidently meaningless' seems to defy logic. You can reply: 'But that can't be true, because those words would also be meaningless, and fail to communicate, and they quite plainly do not.' But if he replies with a shrug and a yawn – as Beckett does – it is difficult to go on arguing.

Or at least, it is hard to see how to begin contradicting it. To the comment: 'Well I don't think so,' the pessimist replies: 'No, you are still suffering from the optimistic illusion – you don't see as deeply as I do.'

Now as we have seen, literary pessimism began with the Romantics – specifically with Byron's rebel hero Manfred (1816), who stands on a mountain top and shakes his fist at the sky.

You can find the essence of pessimism in a remark made by the hero of Senancour's *Obermann*, a famous 19th-century novel about a sensitive recluse: 'The rain depresses me, yet the sunlight strikes me as pointless.' Here we can see the problem. He is suffering from Auden's 'life failure', as discussed in chapter one.

Around the turn of the century, two Russian writers went to extremes of pessimism. Leonid Andreyev wrote a whole series of novels and stories to demonstrate that life is grotesquely senseless, while in his novel *Breaking Point*, Mikhail Artsybashev actually makes *all* the central characters commit suicide.

The most massive attempt to create a philosophy of pessimism is Schopenhauer's *World as Will and Idea*. Schopenhauer's main argument is that human beings are always experiencing powerful desires, yet when they get what they want, they quickly lose interest. (Shakespeare said much the same thing.) Schopenhauer sees us all as driven by short-term emotions that really amount to illusions, and which leave us empty and drained, facing the sheer grotesque stupidity of the universe.

Yet note one thing: although Schopenhauer and Beckett seem to feel that life is about as bad as it can be, neither of them would dream of putting his hand in the fire. They are pragmatic enough to know that life with a burnt hand is a great deal worse than life without one.

Now the truth is that we all swing between extremes of optimism and pessimism. When we are bubbling with energy and looking forward to some pleasant experience, it seems self-evident that life is wonderful. When we get tired, it suddenly begins to seem obvious that all effort is a waste of time. It is as if an invisible weight oppressed our spirits. In a lovely poem called 'Dejection – An Ode', Coleridge writes about gazing at the moon and the stars, and adds:

I see them all, so excellently fair,
I *see*, not *feel*, how beautiful they are.'

The problem is obviously a *feeling* – or rather, lack of feeling.

In my teens I developed a rather useful image to explain what happens when we become bored. My school was a Secondary Technical School, which meant that we could take subjects like engineering, bookbinding and hosiery. In the latter, we could learn to make stockings and scarves.

These were knitted on 'flat-bed' machines, in which two beds of needles, at right angles to one another, rose in turn as a cam holding the wool was passed under them. Each journey of the cam knitted a single row of stitches, and the scarf emerged from underneath the machine. But the wool had to be prevented from climbing up the needles, and so the scarf had to be pulled down towards the floor by weights. If we got carried away, and these weights were allowed to reach the floor, the wool instantly climbed up over the needles and created a hopeless tangle.

I was struck by the fact that human beings also need a kind of 'weight on the needles' in order to operate at their full potential. This weight – in other words a sense of purpose or urgency – prevents our minds from becoming lazy and confused and inefficient. I made this discovery when I was about 11 years old, at the same time as I became fascinated by science. I began writing a book, which I called *A Manual of General Science*, in which I attempted a basic summary of all the scientific knowledge of the world, and which included physics, inorganic chemistry, astronomy, geology, and even (in a later volume) philosophy. I had never enjoyed myself so much in my life. This saved me from the sense of boredom and pointlessness that afflicts so many teenagers and, in due course, led me to become a writer.

In an essay called 'The Revolver in the Corner Cupboard', Graham Greene describes how, as a teenager, boredom led him to drift into an 'affectless' state (as psychologists call it). He would look at something that others described as beautiful, and would see, visually, that it was beautiful; but he would feel nothing whatever – just a kind of grey dullness inside.

In this state, Greene found a revolver belonging to his brother, and went out onto the Berkhamsted Common and played Russian roulette – he put one bullet in it, spun the chambers, then pointed it at his head and pulled the trigger. When there was just a click, he describes experiencing an overwhelming feeling of joy and relief. 'It was as if a light had been turned on … and I felt that life contained an infinite number of possibilities.' In other words, the shock induced an episode of mini-cosmic consciousness.

But the really interesting phrase is: 'It was as if a light had been turned on.' If you go into a dark room and turn on the light, you see *what was there all the time*. In the same way, in *The Lawless Roads*, Greene admits that some situation of crisis 'induced in me something I had not even suspected – a love of life.'

And his priest in *The Power and the Glory*, on the point of being shot by a firing squad, suddenly realizes: 'It would have been so *easy* to be a saint.'

If you go into an art gallery that is badly lit, you can't see the pictures properly. Yet you don't declare that they are therefore bad pictures. This is what the pessimistic philosopher is asserting about life.

Edmund Husserl grasped the basic answer to these mood-swings when he recognized that *consciousness is intentional*. When you 'see' something, it doesn't just walk in through your eyes. You have to fire your attention at it, like an arrow. If you look at your watch without this act of 'intentionality' (i.e. absent-mindedly) you don't see the time, and you have to look again. (I shall return to Husserl later.)

When Greene said that he saw that life contained an infinite number of possibilities, he meant that he felt free to choose between them. Tiredness diminishes our consciousness of freedom, and extreme tiredness – combined with depression or 'negative feedback' – makes us feel that there are no possibilities, that freedom is an illusion.

The answer, as I came to realize in the hosiery class, lies in seeking some purpose that provides a 'weight on the needles'.

In *The Myth of Sisyphus*, Camus asserts that the most funda-mental problem of man is whether we all ought to commit suicide. He states his feeling that life is basically 'absurd' (i.e. mean-ingless) and explains what he means when he says that we go to work, come home, go to work, come home, Monday, Tuesday, Wednesday, etc, until one day, the consciousness of 'the Absurd' dawns upon us. Clearly, all that he means is that when we suddenly feel tired and discouraged, life seems futile (Sartre calls it 'nausea').

But then, when we get into this state, we are simply failing to acknowledge what Harley Granville-Barker calls (in his play of that name) 'the secret life'. When Graham Greene pulled the trigger, he was suddenly flooded with the secret life. This is what Chesterton calls 'absurd good news'. It is the recognition of freedom.

Samuel Beckett remarked that, as a young man, he stayed in bed all day because he couldn't see any reason for getting up. This reveals clearly that his pessimism is closely connected with lack of energy. Similarly, T S Eliot suffered from deep depressions about his disastrous first marriage and, added to his natural tendency to aesthetic 'world rejection', this produced *The Waste Land* and *The Hollow Men*.

I would suggest that in order to understand that nature of freedom, we need first of all to look more carefully at the 'mechanisms of despair'.

The first thing to understand is that we are quite literally speaking of a 'mechanism'. Each of us has a robot inside us who acts as a kind of valet. When I learn something new – like driving a car or how to type – I have to do it painfully and consciously. But my robot valet soon takes over, and proceeds to type or drive the car far more efficiently than 'I' could. He will drive me home when I am tired, and I can't even remember the journey.

The trouble is that he not only takes over tasks I want him to do, like driving and talking French. He also takes over things I *don't* want him to do. I listen to a symphony and am deeply moved; the tenth time I listen, the robot is listening too and I don't enjoy it as much. I like to joke that I have even caught him making love to my wife. This robot is what Gurdjieff means when he says we are machines. He tried to devise methods of forcing his pupils to make far more effort, to foil the robot. But he was rather pessimistic about our chance of defeating it permanently. In order to do this, the mind would have to develop a rock-like solidness that he calls 'essence'.

This leads me to one of my own central insights. You might say that, in our normal healthy state we are roughly 50 per cent 'robot', and 50 per cent 'real you'. When I am tired and low, I become 51 per cent robot and only 49 per cent 'real me'. On the other hand, when I am happy and full of energy, I am 49 per cent robot, and 51 per cent 'real me'.

Now consider what happens if I am so permanently tired that my *normal* condition is only 49 per cent 'real me' and 51 per cent robot. Because I see the world as a duller place, I cease to make so much effort, so my vital batteries get low. This makes it look duller still, and makes effort seem even more pointless. If I am not careful, I go into 'negative feedback', when I become 55 per cent robot and only 45 per cent 'real me'. This is a highly dangerous state, because I now feel so low that all effort seems pointless, and I may slide downhill into mental illness – such as catatonia – and become a kind of vegetable.

On the other hand, if I use the insight of my optimistic moods – when I am 51 per cent 'real me' – to keep me at a high level of drive and optimism, I may achieve states in which I am 52 or 53 per cent 'real me'. This is what had happened to Maslow's 'peakers'.

It is also immensely important not to attach too much importance to temporary setbacks, and above all, to avoid the stupid habit of allowing ourselves, when discouraged, to start looking into the future and seeing it as a series of impending disasters and defeats. Ninety per cent of our problems are self-created. This is what the Hindu scripture means by 'the mind is the slayer of the real.'

In *The Brothers Karamazov*, Dostoevsky makes Ivan say that life is so cruel that he just wants to give God back his entrance ticket. Yet he also makes Alyosha say: 'There is a strength to overcome *anything*.' Ivan's gloomy view is basically a worm's-eye view. Yet we can also see that it is possible to achieve a bird's-eye view that would be *permanent*. In short, we have proved – mathematically, so to speak – the possibility of that next step in evolution, in which we permanently reach a higher stage.

I have another useful concept that explains what goes wrong with us when we are tired. I call it the 'What-is-worth-the-effort level' ('Whittle' for short, although the letters don't quite match-up). When you have a low 'Whittle threshold', you feel that nothing is worth doing. On the other hand, people with a high Whittle threshold are interested in everything, and life strikes them as self-evidently fascinating. From what has been said above, we can see that Samuel Beckett is simply a man with a low Whittle threshold, and that what he is 'saying' has no validity whatsoever.

Since Beckett is the most celebrated of modern pessimists, let me use him as an example of the way the mechanism works.

To begin with, his work after *Endgame* (1955) shows a writer who is getting closer and closer to total non-communication. You get the feeling that he might begin one of his later writings, like his last novel *How It Is (1961)*: 'Warning: this work is not intended to communicate. Please put it down and go away.'

Which raises the question: if he wants us to go away, why is he writing and then publishing his work? How could any sane writer get himself into this illogical and untenable position?

Beckett was born in Dublin in 1906 into a warm and affectionate middle-class family. His father was a successful estate agent who hoped his sons would follow him into the business. The notion left Beckett paralysed with boredom. He was by nature indolent, shy and introverted, so even his family's second choice, an academic career, failed to appeal. He spent some time in Germany, where he fell in love with a cousin named Peggy – who became his mistress but tired of his laziness and found someone else – then went to Paris and met James Joyce, who treated him as his 'gofer', then, for want of anything better to do, he returned to Dublin and became a layabout, living on his family and drinking large amounts of stout. Finally, to avoid being nagged about what he wanted to do with his life, he declared he intended to become a writer, and produced a number of poems, including one called 'Whoroscope', which became his first publication.

At this point Beckett's father died of a heart attack. Beckett received a small allowance as his share of the will, and continued to live at home and suffer from a boredom and frustration that finally brought on panic attacks and a breakdown in health. He remained depressed for years, and eventually went to live in London where he could receive treatment from a Jungian psychotherapist, which convinced him that he had only been partially born, and that as a consequence his mental development had remained lopsided.

He returned to Paris, where Joyce's daughter Lucia fell in love with him, but he told her that he was 'dead inside and had no feelings'. Her pursuit of him – and his frantic flight – led to a temporary break with Joyce.

His first novel *Murphy*, the final outcome of years of work (and inability to work) is about a feckless but literate young Irishman who lives in London and spends most of his time sitting in a rocking chair, since there seems no point in standing up. He likes to take off all his clothes and tie himself in the chair, a fairly obvious symbol of his desire to return to the womb. Then he finds a job in a private nursing home and is finally happy among mental patients who strike him as saner than the people outside. Beckett finally gets rid of his hero by killing him off in an absurd accident that might just be suicide.

The book was rejected more than 40 times before being accepted. Predictably, it failed to make the impression Beckett expected.

Anyone who has read Deirdre Bair's biography will recognize that Beckett's problems sprang from being born into a reasonably well-off family who could support him while he nursed his deep disinclination to choose any course of action. His kind of boredom is suffered by many teenagers, probably a majority, but being born into circumstances that allowed him to go on indulging it into his thirties meant that he wasted most of his early life in the state the saints used to call *accidia*, or spiritual apathy. And he would have undoubtedly continued to suffer from it for the rest of his days if the beginning of the Second World War had not turned his life upside down. But by that time Beckett was simply too old – at 32 – to change his ways.

Back in Paris, Beckett was determined to remain there. He was able to stay on in France, since he was an Irishman. He became a member of the Resistance, microfilming information and transmitting it to London by radio. There can be little doubt that these

activities had a tonic effect on Beckett, since the danger from the
Gestapo and their informers was constant. (We have noted that the
same thing happened to Sartre.) Beckett's whole group was
eventually betrayed by a traitorous priest, and Beckett had to go on
the run. Finally, with his mistress Suzanne, a nurse seven years his
senior, he escaped to the Vichy zone. They settled in the village of
Rousillon in the Vaucluse region, but in due course, this became
as much a prison as his home in Dublin had been, and he began
to suffer the familiar sense of being trapped.

Deirdre Bair remarks about this period: 'In his own life,
Beckett was deeply afraid that lack of structure in his daily existence would have serious consequences for his mental stability,
as it had in the past. He was adept in recognising the symptoms of
disintegration that beset him before a period of depression …'
On the verge of breakdown, he again began to write, this time a
novel called *Watt,* the narrative of a schizophrenic patient in
a madhouse, which has an air of Kafkaesque unreality.

This would remain Beckett's problem. He was pathologically
shy and socially awkward, and the wealthy art collector Peggy
Guggenheim, who became his mistress, spoke about his 'enormous
green eyes that never looked at you'. During a day they spent in
bed he told her that he regarded Céline's *Journey to the End of
Night* – undoubtedly one of the most nihilistic works in all
literature -- as the greatest novel ever written. Discussing the anti-
Soviet pamphlet Céline had written after a visit to Russia, Beckett
said that he felt politics was a waste of time, and that he accepted
life fatalistically. When she lent him Goncharov's *Oblomov,* he
instantly saw his own likeness in the passive hero who has

difficulty in getting out of bed. Guggenheim adds that he was drunk all the time.

Beckett's pessimism and depression reached a kind of climax on a visit to Dublin soon after the war. One March evening in 1946, a long walk had taken him to Dun Laoghaire pier, where a winter storm was in progress. There he had his 'revelation'. A television programme on Beckett expressed it: 'Where others had sought enrichment, he would keep impoverishment. It was like resolving to go naked ...'

In *Krapp's Last Tape* the character expresses it: 'What I saw then was that the assumption I had been going on all my life, namely ... [Beckett's leader dots] clear to me at last that the dark I have been fighting off all this time is in reality ... my most unshatterable association till my dying day'.

For all practical purposes, Beckett had decided that 'the dark he had been fighting off' would become the subject of his future work.

In other words, Beckett was saying that since he was incapable of escaping from depression, he would stop struggling with it, and instead make it his starting point. Instead of treating his sense of meaninglessness with a kind of ironic humour, as in *Murphy* and *Watt*, he would, so to speak, go on the attack, as Céline did, and denounce life as a nightmare.

It was, of course, a technique that had already been utilized by Kafka, so the word Kafkaesque has come to mean a tangle of dream-like complications, in the midst of which the individual feels helpless. This is why Kafka irritates his detractors – like the critic Edmund Wilson – who accused him of dramatizing his own weakness and immaturity as if they are a part of the human condition.

That criticism certainly applies to the novel that Beckett began on his return to Paris in 1947. *Molloy* and its two successors are nothing if not Kafkaesque. It opens with a monologue by a confused schizophrenic cripple, who says he is in his mother's room but doesn't know how he got there. All he wants, he explains, is to finish dying. He then tells how he set out on a journey on a bicycle, with his crutches strapped to it. There follows a rambling and disconnected narrative in which nothing much happens, except that he runs over a dog, goes to live with the lady who rescues him from an angry crowd, then leaves her because he feels she is trying to take over his life.

In a forest he meets a friendly charcoal burner and hits him on the head with his crutch and kicks him when he is unconscious. Then, using his crutches as grapnels he drags himself along the ground until he falls into a ditch, from which someone rescues him and takes him to his mother's room. His attitude towards the world is clearly one of hostility approaching paranoia.

In its second part, the focus of *Molloy* shifts to a private detective called Moran, whose style is altogether more brisk and purposeful. 'It is midnight. The rain is beating on the windows.' However, the reader's relief is short-lived as Moran goes on to tell a tale just as dreamlike as Molloy's. Apparently he has been sent to search for and report on Molloy by the boss of his agency, whose name is Youdi. He sets off walking across the countryside with his son Jacques, but his knee is soon stricken (Beckett seems to have an obsession with crippled characters), and he sends Jacques off to the nearest town to buy a bicycle. Alone, Moran seizes the opportunity to masturbate. (Masturbation plays a recurrent part in the trilogy; in a world drained of motive, sex seems to be the last instinct to survive.) Jacques is absent for three days, and during this time a man carrying a club asks for bread, which Moran gives him. Moran then makes himself a club. When a short man asks if a man with a club has passed that way, Moran denies it, then beats the newcomer to death.

His son returns with a bicycle and they set off, with Moran on the carrier. Moran explains: 'I shall not tell of the obstacles we had to surmount, the fiends we had to circumvent, the misdemeanours of the son, the disintegrations of the father. It was my intention, almost my desire, to tell of these things … Now the intention is dead'.

He has a quarrel with his son, who leaves. Then he receives a note telling him to return home. When he gets there, his place is ruined and the hens and bees are dead. By now he is hearing voices. Finally he writes his report – the novel itself – which begins: 'It is midnight. The rain is beating on the windows', and adds: 'It was not midnight. It was not raining.'

It is hard for the reader, who has just read 176 pages, not to feel *Molloy* is simply too long, and the occasional rewards it offers by way of zany comments and non sequiturs ('I was saying I would not relate all the vicissitudes of the journey from my country to Molloy's, for the simple reason that I do not intend to …') too infrequent and not funny enough.

In the second novel, *Malone Dies*, the narrator, a dying man, lives in a room like the inside of a skull. Again, nothing much happens, except that the old woman who brings him soup and empties his pot stops coming, so he will presumably starve to death, and a stranger (the undertaker?) comes to stare at him.

At this point in his career as a novelist, Beckett felt exhausted and bored, and decided to write a play as a change of pace.

Before *Molloy* he had written a fragment of a novel called *Mercier and Camier*. These are two vagabonds, who drift into an endless quest for something or other, and Beckett was able to transport chunks of their pointless but amusing dialogue straight into the new play, *Waiting for Godot*.

Its two tramps, who seem to owe something to Laurel and Hardy, stand in the middle of a bleak wilderness, under a bare tree, waiting to meet someone called Godot, not even sure if they are in the right place.

By giving them a mock-heroic quality which contrasts with their filthy rags, Beckett makes them amusing. Estragon spends the first few minutes of the play alone, trying to pull off his boot. He gives up in exhaustion, saying, 'Nothing to be done.' His friend Vladimir enters with a Napoleonic stride, saying, 'I'm beginning to come round to that opinion. All my life I've tried to put it from me, saying "Vladimir, be reasonable, you haven't yet tried everything." And I resumed the struggle.'

They might be two professors walking across the lawn of the Sorbonne. Then Estragon gets his boot off, peers inside it, then declines to put it back on, saying he will air it for a bit. Vladimir looks inside his hat, knocks on it, blows into it, then puts it on again. It is the contrast between their down-and-out status and their talk of reason that makes the play funny.

Somehow they get into a theological discussion about the two thieves on the cross, and the disparities between the four gospels, and as Estragon emphasizes his boredom by saying with exaggerated enthusiasm, 'I find this really most extraordinarily interesting,' his resemblance to a professor becomes unmistakable.

A point comes where boredom leads one of them to suggest: 'What about hanging ourselves?' He appears to be suggesting that this will result in ejaculation, and the other becomes excited at the idea and says, 'Let's hang ourselves immediately.' Then it strikes them that if one hangs himself and the other fails, one of them will be left alone. So they abandon another possible source of entertainment.

Beckett sustains the interest by making sure any suggestion of boredom is avoided; no matter how dull the subject, the tramps discuss it earnestly, as if it is a matter of life and death. He has another interesting trick, first deployed in the early novel *Watt*, where the flat, repetitive prose moves forward with incredible slowness, and the humour depends upon the grotesqueness of things seen in slow motion. ('Mr Hackett decided, after some moments, that if the [couple] were waiting for a tram they had been doing so for some time. For the lady held the gentleman by the ears, and the gentleman's hand was on the lady's thigh, and the lady's tongue was in the gentleman's mouth.') Like a record played at a fraction of its proper speed, this gives normal events, such as conversation, an offbeat flavour which is oddly surreal. In *Godot*, long and frequent pauses in the conversation serve a similar purpose.

Just as the audience is beginning to wonder how long this can go on, a horrible shriek electrifies everyone, and the tramps flee in panic. A man staggers on stage with a long rope round his neck, carrying a heavy bag and a picnic basket. Behind him comes his master Pozzo, cracking a whip. Overweight, noisy and bullying, we suspect Pozzo is intended as a symbol of the capitalist class, and his servant Lucky represents the downtrodden workers. Indeed, Pozzo proves to be the owner of all the land thereabouts. He is inclined to be condescendingly friendly. 'Yes, gentleman, I cannot go for long without the society of my likes. (*He puts on his glasses and looks at the two likes.*) Even when the likeness is an imperfect one. (*He takes off his glasses.*)' He makes Lucky give him the picnic hamper, and proceeds to eat a large meal with wine. The two tramps examine Lucky with pity, but Lucky repays a friendly overture by kicking Estragon on the shin and almost crippling him. In the long scene that follows, Lucky dances (briefly) and thinks aloud (at breakneck speed in a meaningless monologue). And when finally Pozzo and Lucky leave, Vladimir says, 'That passed the time,' and Estragon replies, 'It would have passed anyway.'

'Let's go,' says Estragon.

'We can't.'

'Why not?'

'We're waiting for Godot'.

At last a boy appears, to deliver a message that Mr Godot will come tomorrow.

As the tramps begin to move off, Estragon raises the question of whether they ought to separate. But both agree that it is too late.

'Shall we go?' asks Estragon, and Vladimir agrees, 'Yes, let's go.' But they make no move as the curtain descends.

The second act is virtually a repetition of the first, except that when Pozzo reappears he is blind, and is being led by Lucky. And it ends in the same way, with Vladimir saying 'Shall we go?' and then neither of them moving.*Godot* is Beckett's best work, the one in which he got the balance between humour and seriousness exactly right; something he would never achieve again. The Molloy trilogy makes us aware of how easily he could cross the line from humour and imagination to a kind of bleak self-pity that seems designed to induce either torpor or derision. And the last part of the trilogy, *The Unnamable*, demonstrates how easily that uncertain balance could tilt him into creative sterility.

It was started in 1948, soon after Beckett finished *Godot*. It is a solipsistic monologue from an unidentified character who seems to be looking forward to his extinction. It is Beckett's most uncompromisingly desolate work. A disembodied voice – although a mention of his crutches hints at Molloy – simply talks on into the darkness, without paragraphs. There are not even anecdotes. The character sits in a shallow container, completely paralysed, and we gather through the obscurity of the monologue that he will lose his limbs, and end in a large pot full of sawdust outside a French restaurant specializing in turnips in gravy. The book ends: 'I don't know, I'll never know, in the silence you don't know, you must go on, I can't go on, I'll go on.'

But in one significant paragraph, the narrator says:

> All these Murphys, Molloys and Malones do not fool
> me. They have made me waste my time, suffer for
> nothing, speak of them when, in order to stop
> speaking, I should have spoken of me and of
> me alone.

In other words, Beckett is telling us that he has been wasting his time writing fiction. What he should have done is to speak to the reader directly. Clearly, Beckett has become rather disoriented about this whole enterprise of communication. And, as we shall see, this confusion represents a fatal watershed in his work.

For surely, the relation of any artist to his audience is basically that of a puppet showman to the children he is entertaining. The audience knows perfectly well that this is a convention, that the puppets are not real people, that there is a man hidden behind the curtain. But so long as the showman sticks to his side of the bargain and pretends that Punch and Judy are real, the audience will go on watching. But if the showman suddenly sticks his head into the proscenium and declares that he is wasting his time being Punch and Judy, and he is now going to talk about himself, the audience will melt away.

This is more or less how the reader feels as he listens to the complaints of the Unnamable. For it makes the reader aware of the fragility of the whole fictional enterprise, and that all that has happened in the 418 pages of the trilogy is that the author has made less and less effort to communicate, until he has finally given up altogether, apparently out of profound boredom or fatigue.

Premiered finally in November 1953, *Waiting for Godot* was, of course, the success that changed Beckett's life. But its original success was due to scandal rather than appreciation. Many people felt that it was an outrage that they should be asked to sit through a play 'in which,' as one critic put it, 'nothing happens, twice.' It was like Chekhov, only worse. Surely it was some kind of hoax? And the liveliness, and occasional bitterness, of the discussion, kept the Théâtre de Babylone full until Beckett became aware that at last, at the age of 47, he was famous.

He owed this to Suzanne. Beckett's typical boredom and apathy had almost prevented *Godot* reaching the stage. After finishing it in January 1949, he soon collapsed into a state of will-lesssness, spending day after day in bed, and it was Suzanne who tried to peddle his work. It had been her idea to approach Roger Blin, a director who had been a friend of Antonin Artaud. Blin liked it, and he and Beckett met during the early summer of 1950. Blin dropped his idea of performing it in a circus as being too expensive.

In late October, Suzanne took the *Molloy* trilogy along to a French publisher, Editions de Minuit, which had started up as an underground press during the war, publishing a famous novel about the Resistance, *The Silence of the Sea*, by Jean Bruller, who wrote as Vercors. Editions de Minuit was interested in avant garde writing but, at the time Suzanne took Beckett's novels there, was on the point of bankruptcy. The new owner of the firm, Jerome Lindon, had heard of Beckett, possibly as a decorated hero of the Resistance (De Gaulle had given him a medal). He began to read *Molloy*, was intrigued by it, and tried to telephone Beckett the next day, only to learn he had no phone. He summoned Suzanne

—
100

by telegram, and after seeing him she rushed home to tell Beckett that Lindon wanted to publish all three novels. Typically, Beckett was stunned rather than delighted – his normal depression and exhaustion left him little energy to cope with good news. And when he had signed the contract (with an advance of less than £25) he returned home miserable that he would be the cause of Lindon's bankruptcy. In fact, the first two novels sold fairly well on publication in 1951, and were treated with the kind of respect the French show to obscure but worthy intellectual enterprises.

Perhaps unsurprisingly, Beckett experienced a creative blockage after writing *Godot* and *The Unnamable*. After all, *The Unnamable* must have seemed an impossible act to follow. And what of the theatre? How was it possible to go beyond *Godot*? More to the point, why should anyone want to? Was it not a self-contradictory exercise to go on repeating that life was meaningless and futile? For if it was true, why bother to do it? The only logical follow-on would have been to commit suicide as publicly as possible. But this was unlikely. After January 1953, he was rather enjoying being famous. Finally, in December 1955, he began to write the first words of a play that became *Fin de Partie*, or *Endgame*.

Clearly, the characters had to be even more trapped, more hopeless, more doomed, than in *Godot*. But how was that to be done without risking an exaggeration that might invite derision?

Whether Beckett's solution achieves this is an open question.

His first step was to make the central character, Hamm, a blind cripple confined to a wheelchair. On the floor in dustbins are his legless parents, Nagg and Nell. The fourth character, Hamm's adopted son Clov, has something wrong with his legs, so he cannot sit down, and has to walk with stiff legs like a Frankenstein monster. Hamm treats him as a servant, and Clov hates him. Outside, apparently, there is a landscape devoid of nature, as if there has been an atomic disaster.

The insertion of an element of entertainment into this chronicle of disaster was obviously beyond Beckett's powers of invention, so he decided to dispense with it. So when, at the beginning of the play, we hear Clov say, 'Finished, it's finished, nearly finished, it must be nearly finished,' we are back to the end of *The Unnamable*: 'I can't go on.' At this point, Hamm wakes up, yawns repeatedly, and asks, 'Can there be misery loftier than mine?' Then he asks the time. 'The same as usual,' says Clov. And he and Hamm proceed to bicker.

'Why don't you kill me?'

'I don't know the combination of the larder.'

(*Pause*)

'Go and get two bicycle-wheels.'

'There are no more bicycle-wheels.'

'What have you done with your bicycle?'

'I never had a bicycle'.

'The thing is impossible.'

'When there were still bicycles I wept to have one. I crawled at your feet. You told me to get out to hell. Now there are none.'

The parents wake up and begin to reminisce about a long-past holiday when they crashed a tandem. Clearly, they still love one another. But Hamm asks them to shut up because they are keeping him awake with their chatter.

In *Endgame* there are no diversions, like the entrance of Pozzo and Lucky. Nothing of note happens, except that Clov hits Hamm on the head with a toy dog, to which Hamm responds, 'If you must hit me, hit me with an axe.'

After this, Clov changes into his outdoor clothes and stands by the door, prepared to leave, as Hamm goes into a final soliloquy, in which he promises to speak no more. Then he covers his face with his handkerchief as the curtain comes down.

Unsurprisingly, no Paris management was willing to stage the play. The London performances I saw in 1957 (in French) and 1958 (in English) were the first. It seemed to me then that *Endgame* was a simple miscalculation on the part of its author, who had transformed himself from a humorist into a preacher. I felt as Tolstoy did about Leonid Andreyev: 'He keeps shouting Boo, but he doesn't scare me.'

In the half-century since then, my view has not changed even minimally, in the face of eminent critics like Al Alvarez and Harold Bloom, who regard it as a masterpiece. I still feel that to present a play in which nothing happens is like inviting guests to dinner with empty plates.

This impression has persisted in the face of later works, like *Come and Go* (three minutes), *Breath* (35 seconds) and *Not I* (15 minutes). In *Breath*, the light comes on slowly to reveal a stage that is empty except for items of rubbish, and a sound of breathing. Then the light dims slowly until the stage is again in darkness. (Ironically, this was presented as the opening 'sketch' of Tynan's sex review *Oh Calcutta!*, as if Beckett was getting his own back for that parody of *Endgame*.) In *Not I* a spotlit mouth utters in the darkness a fragmented monologue in which the words are separated by leader dots: 'out ... into this world ... this world ... tiny little thing ... before its time ... in a godfor- ... what? ... girl ... yes ... tiny little girl,' and which includes such lines as 'a merciful ... (*brief laugh*) ... God ... (*good laugh*).'

This latter makes clear, as far as anything can, what Beckett regards as the basic problem of human existence. Life is apparently meaningless and repetitive. ('The sun shone, having no alternative, on the nothing new.') Why do intelligent people not see this? Because they make the false assumption that God exists, or some equivalent assumption, such as that we are in the world for a reason. If this illusion could be dispelled by a flash of enlightenment, we would then experience a state of clear-sighted indifference. And in that case, we would agree that the works of Samuel Beckett present a fair and undistorted picture of this world we have been born into.

But what if, like me, we feel that Beckett's pessimism is based upon certain assumptions that we do not share? One of these can be pinpointed in *Endgame*, in a speech by Nagg in which he tells the story of the tailor. An Englishman orders a pair of trousers from a tailor, who tells him to return in four days. When he returns the tailor tells him he has made a mess of the seat and to return in a week. As this goes on until the spring, the angry customer finally shouts: 'God made the world in six days, and you haven't finished my trousers in three months.' 'But my dear sir,' says the tailor, 'look at the world, then look at my trousers.'

The world, says Beckett, is a mess. Who is to blame? Clearly, its maker. This is Beckett's basic obsession, his King Charles' head, and it is possible to make a list of his disparaging references to God, from Murphy's 'What but an imperfect sense of humour could have made such a mess of chaos?' to Hamm's 'The bastard! He doesn't exist.' Like Dostoevsky's Ivan Karamazov, Beckett proposes to give God back his entrance ticket. However, Dostoevsky offers his own answer, in the scene where Alyosha emerges from his state of despair to experience an ecstatic vision of the night and the stars: 'There seemed to be threads from all these innumerable worlds of God, linking his soul to them ...'

Now Beckett specifically disclaims 'vision'. In Clov's final soliloquy he says, 'I say to myself the the earth is extinguished, though I never saw it lit.' When Hamm asks Clov if he ever had an instant of happiness, he answers 'Not to my knowledge.' Beckett characters know nothing of peak experiences. They are stuck firmly in the Ecclesiastes effect, the feeling that 'all is vanity'.

What has led them to this conclusion? Beckett's tailor has told us the answer: 'Look at the world, then look at my trousers.' Human beings and the world they live in are radically unsuited to one another.

In a short playlet called *Act Without Words*, which preceded *Fin de Partie* at the Court, the argument is elaborated. A man is hurled on to the desert-like stage from the wings, and when he tries to return, is hurled back. Obviously, this is man being 'thrown' – as Heidegger would say – into the world. He tries leaving from the other side, and is again hurled back. But as he sits there, staring in front of him, a small tree is lowered from above. When he notices it, he goes and sits in its shade. It looks as if fate means well by him after all. Then the tree closes like an umbrella, dispelling that notion.

A carafe of water descends but, when he approaches it, rises out of reach. Then a huge cube descends. He stands on it but the water is still beyond his reach. Then a second, smaller, cube descends. He places it on top of the other and tries to reach the water. The carafe rises beyond his reach. Next a knotted rope descends but, when he tries climbing it, suddenly rises into the air, so he lets go in alarm and falls to earth. The carafe of water is also pulled up and disappears.

The man contemplates suicide with a pair of scissors that have appeared from above. But while he is thinking about it, they also vanish. Someone 'up there' is obviously enjoying a joke at his expense. So he lies on the ground and declines to move, even when the carafe is dangled within easy reach. The carafe then disappears, and so does the tree. The man lies there and refuses to move. Curtain.

One thing is clear. Beckett is saying that our world is not just indifferent to human beings. It is actively malicious. Which would seem to imply that he is not an objective observer, but is getting his emotions – and self-pity – involved. In other words, he cannot be regarded as trustworthy.

The same inner-contradiction repeatedly undermines the work of his contemporary Albert Camus. In *L'Etranger*, the central character, Meursault, is involved in the accidental shooting of an Arab on the beach. Because it had been noticed by the mourners that he did not cry at his mother's funeral, he is accused of being cold-blooded and heartless, and condemned to death. But since Meursault speaks about the 'benign indifference' of the universe, we assume his fate is merely a matter of tragic irony. Why, in that case, does Meursault recount the story of a sailor who returns home after 25 years, and in order to give his mother and sister a pleasant surprise, does not reveal his identity – with the result that they murder him for his money before realizing what they have done, and killing themselves. To underline the point, Camus used the same plot in his play *Le Malentendu* (*Cross-purposes*). This is not a benignly indifferent universe; it is actively hostile.

This, I would argue, goes beyond his existentialist remit. Existentialism is supposed to make no assumptions about the world, and to suggest that we are the 'sports of circumstance' – as Thomas Hardy puts it – is a religious assumption in disguise.

In fact, Camus retreated from his nihilism in *The Plague*. Sartre's subsequent 'commitment' to combining existentialism and Marxism also superseded the nihilism of *Being and Nothingness*. But for Beckett, having committed himself to the total negativity of *The Unnamable* and *Endgame*, there could be no second thoughts. In a letter of 1959, Beckett recognized that he was trapped. '… the hole I have got myself into now is as "dumb of all light" as the 5th canto of Hell and by God no love.' And for the rest of his life the predicaments of his central characters – in dustbins, in urns, lying in mud or buried in sand – reflect his total rejection of hope. Beckett is like a man who has sentenced himself to life imprisonment.

In 1969, fate demonstrated a capacity for ironic humour when Beckett was awarded the Nobel Prize for Literature. Suzanne, who took the phone call from the Swedish Academy, greeted the news with the comment: 'Quelle catastrophe!' They hastened to a small village in Tunisia to hide. When reporters eventually found him there, he agreed to meet with them only on condition they asked no questions.

The presentation speech was made by Karl Ragnar Gierow, poet and critic, who had cast the deciding vote. Oddly enough, he selected the play *Happy Days* as the second of Beckett's 'two masterpieces', the first being, of course, *Godot*. This is a play in which a woman, buried first up to her waist and then to her neck, in sand, apparently fails to notice her predicament, and chatters away cheerfully to her husband, even declaring at one point, 'This *is* a happy day!' The implication seems to be that, like most people, she is too stupid to realize she is trapped.

Gierow describes Beckett's philosophy as 'a negativism that cannot desist from descending to the depths'. It is only in the depths, he says, that pessimism can work its miracles. 'Because what does one get when a negative is printed? A positive, a clarification with black proving to be the light of day.' Its name, he says, is fellow-feeling, charity. And he reached a climax with: 'From that position, in the realms of annihilation, rises the writing of Samuel Beckett like a miserere for all mankind, its muffled minor key sounding liberation to the oppressed, and comfort to those in need.' Here Beckett is represented as a kindly humanist trying to bestow comfort on his fellow men. If that is true, the audience should leave *Endgame* feeling purged and reconciled to life.

As if to make sure that no one ever again accused him of wanting to liberate the oppressed or comfort those in need, Beckett made sure that from then on, works like *Lessness* (1969), *The Lost Ones* (1970), *Fizzles* (1973), *As the Story Was Told* (1973) and *The*

Cliff (1975) were bleak, comfortless and incomprehensible.

Gierow's attempt at an apologia for Beckett only emphasizes the strength of the case against him. The Russian philosopher Leo Shestov said of Chekhov: 'Stubbornly, despondently, monotonously, during his entire period of literary activity, Chekhov did one thing only: in one way or another he killed human hopes.' Whether or not this is true of the kindly and compassionate Chekhov, it is certainly true of Beckett. To say that, after all, his works did no harm would be an evasion. To kill hope *is* to do harm. *The Unnamable* and *Endgame* were conceived out of despair, and their aim is to make others share it.

Now in fact, the comparison with Chekhov is enlightening. For while it is true that many of Chekhov's main characters – Uncle Vanya, Trigorin, Treplev – tend to be will-less and unhappy, Chekhov himself was firmly convinced that the future of civilization was guaranteed by the advancement of science.

So why were his plays so pessimistic when he himself was an optimist?

The answer is simple. Chekhov was a passive sort of person. So what he believed about the human future is irrelevant. When a passive sort of person is a playwright, he writes about passive people.

The history of existentialism is full of such characters, and all underline the same point. Meursault, the hero of Camus's *L'Etranger*, is essentially passive; he drifts lazily through life, making no effort. And the 'nausea' that paralyses Roquentin, the hero of Sartre's first novel, is based on passivity. In fact, from Kierkegaard onward, Existentialism is essentially passive – about people who find themselves in a world they have not chosen, and want to know what they are doing here. They survey it carefully to see if they can grasp any clues to its underlying meaning, but it gazes back blankly. So they conclude, like Sartre: 'It is meaningless that we live, and meaningless that we die'.

However, let us recollect the case of Maslow's student who ceased to menstruate (page 24). This makes us aware of what happens when someone sinks into long-term passivity and discouragement. The vital batteries go flat and everything becomes meaningless and joyless.

The moral is that before you try to see in the dark you must make sure that the torch batteries are charged.

Which provides us with the clue we need to take us to the next stage of the argument.

Chapter Seven

Absurd Good News

It was Proust who coined the phrase *moments bienheureux,* 'moments of wellbeing'. They are what G K Chesterton meant by 'absurd good news'.

We may recall how, in *Swann's Way,* Proust describes coming home cold and tired, and tasting a little cake dipped in herb tea:

> No sooner had the warm liquid mixed with the crumbs touched my palate than a shudder ran through me and I stopped, intent upon the extraordinary thing that was happening to me. An exquisite pleasure had invaded my senses, something isolated, detached, with no suggestion of its origin. And at once the vicissitudes of life had become indifferent to me, its disasters innocuous, its brevity illusory – this new sensation having had on me the effect which love has of filling me with a precious essence; or rather, this essence was not in me, it was me. I had now ceased to feel mediocre, accidental, mortal …

Several more tastes of the madeleine dipped in tea finally reveal to him that the 'exquisite pleasure' was due to memories of childhood in a little town called Combray, when his Aunt Leonie used to give him a taste of her own madeleine dipped in lime blossom tea.

The *moment bienheureux* is, quite simply, a surge of strength and power. It is, in short, what I refer to, in the title of this book, as 'power consciousness'. Proust would certainly have demurred at this term, but nevertheless, that is what it is. Proust would have demurred because he did not see himself as a 'powerful' person – on the contrary, he thought of himself as an invalid and a hypochondriac – which is why he was doubly surprised by the flash of 'absurd good news'.

Why should the taste of the madeleine bring a feeling of power? Because it brings back clearly an episode in his past, and made him aware that *he is still the same person.* He thinks of himself as a slave of time, its helpless subject, and the moment of power reveals that, in some basic sense, this is untrue. 'The essence was not in me, it was me.'

It is typical of Beckett that, in a slim book on Proust written in 1930, he treats the *moments bienheureux* as little more than an oddity of memory and habit, so although he offers an abbreviated list of the 60-odd such experiences, he concentrates on an incident from *Sodome et Gomorrhe* when, unbuttoning his boot, Marcel is reminded of his grandmother, who died the year before, and suddenly *grasps* that she is dead, something he had so far taken casually for granted. This, of course, involves nothing '*bienheureux*'. For Beckett is not concerned with glimpses of absurd good news, but with man's slavery to time and to slow disintegration.

Proust's hero experiences the same illumination in the final volume, *Time Regained*, when, feeling rather depressed and discouraged, he is on his way to a reception. In the courtyard he steps back to avoid a car and almost loses his balance on an uneven paving stone. Yet once again, 'all my discouragement vanished, and in its place was that same happiness which had been given to me at various epochs of my life …' Once again he is able to remember why he feels so happy: the uneven flagstones have suddenly recalled the uneven paving stones in the Baptistery of St Mark's in Venice. Twice more in the next quarter of an hour he experiences similar flashes of 'magic', once when a servant accidentally knocks a spoon against a plate, reminding him of a railwayman testing wheels with a hammer on the Balbec line, and once more when he wipes his mouth with a napkin, releasing a flash of memory of performing the same action on holiday in Balbec. Brooding once again on this problem, Proust reaches the conclusion that the reason for that odd feeling of 'immortality' is that such experiences occurred 'outside time'. That is to say, he grasps that he himself is, in some important sense, above time. He is experiencing what, in the first chapter of this book, I called 'duo-consciousness', the odd ability to be conscious of two places at once.

This is what produces the flood of delight, the sensation of 'ceasing to feel mediocre, accidental, mortal'. It is the recognition that consciousness is not restricted to the boring, down-to-earth present in which we are all stuck for most of our lives. It can achieve a strange double-focus that can suddenly arouse in us, as Proust says, 'the desire to live which is reborn whenever we become conscious anew of beauty and of happiness'. And Proust might almost have had Beckett in mind when he added: 'And we deliver on life a pessimistic judgement which we suppose to be accurate, for we believed we were taking happiness and beauty into account, whereas in fact we left them out and replaced them by a synthesis in which there is not a single atom of either'.

What gets left out of account is a type of awareness I sometimes refer to as 'holiday consciousness', the feeling children experience when setting out on holiday. Expectation of interesting experiences arouses a flood of energy, 'the secret life', which makes it self-evident that life is marvellously complex and fascinating. And if we compare this with the 'pessimistic judgement' mentioned by Proust, we can see immediately that no relativist argument can undermine it – 'It's impossible to say which is true' – because in a perfectly objective sense, the world around us *is* infinitely varied, and not as monochromatic and narrow as Beckett's universe.

Chapter Eight

The Two Selves

Once we understand its mechanisms, we can see that literary pessimism is, as Proust recognized, quite simply a mistake, a logical error that leaves something important out of account.

But for most of the characters I discussed in *The Outsider* the problem is not so simple. Ivan Karamazov talks about 'giving God back his entrance ticket' because of the horror he feels about human cruelty: for example, a small boy torn to pieces by a pack of dogs set on him by a sadistic landowner.

For Van Gogh, it was a choice between the Eternal Yes of *The Starry Night* and the 'Eternal No' of 'Misery will never end'. In the 20th century, the sheer scale of the political horrors has made us far more conscious of Eternal No.

Having looked at the advocates of Eternal No, let us look more closely at Eternal Yes.

In the *Seven Pillars of Wisdom*, T E Lawrence describes setting out on one of those 'clear dawns that wake up the senses with the sun, while the intellect, tired after the thinking of the night, was yet abed. For an hour or two, on such a morning, the sounds, scents and colours of the world struck man individually and directly, not filtered through or made typical by thought …'

This is obviously the basic 'poetic' mood, the mood in which all poets, from Hesiod to Rupert Brooke, have felt that the world is a miraculous place – like London seen from Westminster Bridge by Wordsworth, 'all bright and glittering in the smokeless air'.

Recent discoveries in 'split-brain physiology' enable us to understand this scientifically.

Even in the 19th century, it was recognized that the two halves of our brains have different functions. The speech function resides in the left half, and doctors observed that people who had suffered damage to the left hemisphere became inarticulate. The right side of the brain is apparently connected with recognition of shapes and patterns, so that an artist who had right-brain damage would lose all artistic talent. One man could not even draw a clover leaf; he put the three leaves of the clover side by side, on the same level.

Yet an artist with left-brain damage only became inarticulate; he was still as good an artist as ever. And an orator with right-brain damage could sound as eloquent as ever, even though he could not draw a clover leaf.

The left brain is also involved in logic and reason – for example, adding up a laundry list or doing a crossword puzzle. The right is involved in such activities as musical appreciation or recognizing faces. In short, you could say that the left is a scientist and the right is an artist.

One of the odd facts of human physiology is that the left side of the body is controlled by the right side of the brain, and vice versa. No one quite knows why this is, except that it probably makes for greater integration. If the left brain controlled the left side and the right brain the right side, there might be 'frontier disputes'; as it is, each has a foot firmly in the other's territory.

The upper part of the brain – the 'cerebral hemispheres' – looks like a walnut with a kind of bridge connecting the two halves. This bridge is a knot of nerves, like telephone cables, called the *corpus callosum,* or commissure. But doctors learned that there are some freaks who possess no commissure yet seem to function perfectly well. This led them to wonder if they could prevent epileptic attacks by severing the commissure, and thus preventing the electrical storm from passing from one side to the other. They tried it on epileptic patients and it seemed to work. The fits were greatly reduced, and the patient seemed to be otherwise unchanged. It led doctors to wonder what the commissure was *for*. Someone suggested it might be for transmitting epileptic seizures; another suggested it might be to stop the brain sagging in the middle.

In the 1950s, experiments in America began to shed light on the problem. Someone noticed that if a 'split-brain' patient knocked against a table with his left side, he didn't seem to notice. It began to emerge that the split-brain operation has the effect of preventing one half of the brain from learning what the other half knows. If a split-brain cat was taught a trick with one eye covered, then required to do it with the other eye covered, it was baffled. It became clear that we literally have two brains.

Moreover, if a split-brain patient is shown an apple with the left visual field and an orange with the right, then asked what he has just seen, he replies: 'Orange.' Asked to write what he has just seen with his left hand, he writes 'Apple.' In one experiment, a split-brain patient who was shown an indecent picture with her right brain blushed; asked why she was blushing, she replied truthfully: 'I don't know.'

The person who was doing the blushing was the one who lived in the right half of her brain. She herself lived in the left half. This is true of all of us (except left-handers, whose brain hemispheres are the other way round). The person you call 'you' lives in the left half – the half that 'copes' with the real world. The person who lives in the right is a stranger.

Where does the 'robot' come into all this? He is obviously not the left hemisphere, which is the everyday conscious 'you'. But equally obviously, he cannot be the right, the 'other you', which is anything but 'automatic'. He must be situated in some other part of the brain – possibly the cerebellum, the huge 'animal brain' that lies below the cerebral hemispheres and is, according to the psychologist Stan Gooch, the home of the unconscious mind. Or perhaps, like memory itself, he has no precise location, but is spread throughout the brain. But this is of no practical importance to what concerns us now.

There are, then, two people living inside your head. You might object that you and I are not split-brain patients. That makes no difference. Mozart once remarked that tunes were always walking into his head fully fledged, and all he had to do was to write them down. Where did they come from? Obviously, the right half of his brain, the 'artist'. Where did they go? The left half of his brain – where Mozart lived. In other words, Mozart was a split-brain patient. And if Mozart was, then so are the rest of us.

The person we call 'I' is the scientist. The 'artist' lives in the shadows, and we are scarcely aware of his existence, except in moods of deep relaxation, or of 'inspiration'.

Now this obviously explains T E Lawrence's problem. What he called his 'thought-riddled nature', which prevented him from relaxing and enjoying life, was his highly dominant left brain. When he set out on the 'clear dawn that wakes up the senses with the sun', everything looked so marvellous because he was seeing the world through his right brain.

But the right brain also seems to have another important function. There is good evidence that it is the source of 'power consciousness'.

A remarkable 19th-century pioneer named Thomson Jay Hudson anticipated the results of modern 'split-brain physiology'. Hudson was a newspaper editor who, in the 1890s, became fascinated by hypnosis, and the extraordinary powers which it seems able to release in hypnotized subjects. He was impressed when a rather stupid young man was 'introduced' by the hypnotist to various dead philosophers, and produced brilliant and profound discourses. Hudson concluded that man has two 'selves', which he called the objective and the subjective mind: one 'copes' with external events, one deals with our inner life. The latter, he became convinced, has extraordinary unrecognized powers.

We can see that modern 'split-brain research' has revealed the basic accuracy of Hudson's theory of the 'two selves'.

The core of Hudson's theory is that the 'second self' possesses almost miraculous powers – he describes how he learned to cure sick people at a distance by projecting 'healing intentions' when on the verge of sleep or waking, and says that, in over a hundred experiments, none were not to some extent successful.

Again, a 19th-century hypnotist named Hansen liked to do a spectacular trick in which a hypnotized subject was told that he would become as stiff as a board. He was then made to lie across two chairs, with his head on one and his heels on the other. Several people would then stand on his chest and stomach, and he would not bend in the middle. What happens is obvious. The hypnotist puts the left brain (the 'everyday self') to sleep, leaving the right wide awake. And the right obviously possesses extraordinary powers.

But if the hypnotist can 'order' your right brain to do these amazing things, why can't *you* (your left-brain self) do the same? Because your right brain wouldn't believe you when you tell it that it can make the body go as stiff as a board – it knows you lack self-confidence. (At least, it *thinks* it knows, because you yourself don't believe you can do it.) *If* you could deliver the order with as much force and conviction as the hypnotist, it would obey you.

But most of us lack that kind of force; like T E Lawrence, we are too undermined by self-doubt. This raises an extremely interesting possibility. If 'you' *knew* you could do it, you could make your 'subjective self' obey the orders. But in order to know you could do it, you would have to see the subjective self obeying your order, and it won't obey your order unless you know you can do it – an apparently unresolvable contradiction that has become known as a 'Catch-22' situation. (In Joseph Heller's novel, someone attempts to simulate insanity to avoid combat – but his desire to avoid combat is regarded as proof of his sanity.)

However, consider what happened to Colonel Olcott, Madame Blavatsky's second-in-command. He found himself in the position where he had to persuade some Hindu patients to believe he had healing powers, so he went through the motions, and they were cured – presumably by self-suggestion. At this point, Olcott realized – to his amazement – that he did have healing powers; he could now feel the energy flowing out of him and producing the cure. His deception had developed into the real thing.

As you read these words, you may (with luck) feel a rising glow of optimism, a feeling: 'Yes, it probably *can* be done.' For words, argument – *knowledge* – can deliver us from the Catch-22 situation. This is one of my fundamental points, indeed, *the* fundamental point. Yes, there *are* DIY methods for inducing PEs and experiences of mini-cosmic consciousness. But when used alone, these are as unimportant as drinking wine or smoking pot. What matters is *the knowledge that lies behind them.* That is where the answer lies.

We might liken the 'two selves' to Laurel and Hardy. Ollie is the objective mind, 'you'. Stan is the subjective mind, the 'hidden you'. But Stan happens to be in control of your energy supply. So if you wake up feeling low and discouraged, you (Ollie) tend to transmit your depression to Stan, who fails to send you energy, which makes you feel lower than ever. This vicious circle is the real cause of most mental illness.

Freud's case of Anna O is an illuminating example. Her real name was Bertha Pappenheim, and Freud's colleague Josef Breuer was treating her for hysterical neurosis. Depression that began with the death of her much-loved father caused her to become a dual personality. Out walking with Breuer she suddenly climbed a tree, but when asked why she had done it, had absolutely no memory of the event. But she would fall into trances in which she talked to herself, and by questioning her 'trance-self', Breuer was finally able to find out what had caused the problem. Sitting by the bedside of her dying father, she had fallen asleep with her arm over the back of a chair, and the arm had 'gone to sleep'. She dreamed she saw a black snake wriggling towards her father, and tried to drive it away, but her arm was paralysed. The next day, she saw in the garden a branch that reminded her of the snake, and the arm became paralysed. A circle of depression and delusion ensued, which Breuer was finally able to cure when he learned the story of her dream-snake.

In terms of Bertha's 'Stan and Ollie', these two aspects of herself had reinforced one another's depression and sense of helplessness until Breuer's discovery of the dream provided him with the key to the situation and enabled him to 'wake her up'.

The case demonstrates that neurosis is a form of self-hypnosis. Beckett's neurosis, dating from the boredom and depression of his Dublin days, gradually took possession of his personality, until his only relief lay in trying to write it out of his system in nightmares like *Molloy*. He is an example of what happens when Stan and Ollie, instead of providing mutual support, only obstruct one another.

When I met Beckett at the Royal Court Theatre in 1957, I was inclined to challenge him and ask how he could justify his pessimism, but he seemed such a nice person that I didn't have the heart. I now see that it would have been pointless anyway.

He would not have had the slightest idea of how he came to think as he did.

As soon as we experience an optimistic state of mind, Stan and Ollie begin to demonstrate what they can do in a more positive relation. This is what happens to a child on Christmas morning. As soon as Ollie wakes up and realizes it is Christmas, he experiences a flash of happiness that sends a positive message to Stan, who promptly responds with a surge of energy. This reinforces Ollie's feeling that today is going to be a good day, and his optimism makes Stan send up still more energy – positive instead of negative feedback. This is reinforced by Christmas music, decorations on the Christmas tree, the smell of roasting turkey and mince pies, until the child experiences a positive state of mind in which he feels surrounded by a cloud of happiness.

Note that when Bucke had his experience of cosmic consciousness (see chapter four), he had spent the evening talking about Shelley, Wordsworth and Whitman with friends (Whitman, especially, is full of the 'bird's eye view'), and so was *intellectually* in a state of optimism. What happened then was a build-up of 'positive feedback', happening in a few seconds – rising happiness causes rising intellectual optimism, which in turns causes another flood of happiness, which reinforces the optimism – and suddenly, such a burst of sheer joy that it made him wonder if something was on fire.

Note also that Ramakrishna's ecstasy as he saw the flock of white birds against the black storm cloud is an example of the same mechanism of mutual reinforcement. Similarly, his vision of the divine mother when he had seized a sword to kill himself involved the same mechanism as Graham Greene's feeling of relief and delight when playing Russian roulette.

But why was Ramakrishna able to revive the experience of *samadhi* at will, while Greene quickly relapsed into his normal gloomy view of existence? The 'Stan and Ollie' theory shows us the answer. Greene was naturally depressed and lacking in self-confidence, so he quickly relapsed into negative feedback, with Stan and Ollie mutually obstructing one another, while Ramakrishna, having learned how to make them cooperate, could induce the vision at will.

This, of course, also explains why Maslow's students kept on having PEs once they began to talk about them to one another. Clearly, this is an insight of staggering importance. Armed with this, we are already halfway to achieving PEs at will.

I personally began to recognize the importance of the Stan–Ollie relationship many decades before I had heard of split-brain physiology. All young writers get moods of 'inspiration' in which they pour down words on to paper and feel they've written a masterpiece. Then they look at it the next morning, and it's *awful* – like squashed flies on the paper. When it's happened several times, you begin to suspect that these marvellous insights *can't* be captured in words, because words are too crude and clumsy. Yet, because you are a writer, you persist. And one day, you re-read what you wrote yesterday, and it's still there. The result is a burst of optimism, the knowledge that it can be done.

When you are writing well, you become conscious that your 'other self' is tossing up ideas and inspirations, while 'you' (the left brain) catch them and turn them into words. And the right is delighted to see how well you've caught its meaning, and says, 'Yes, yes, that's what I meant!', and you say 'Oh thanks!' and proceed to do it even better. Suddenly, it is like a tennis match where both players are in top form, or like two lumberjacks at either end of a double-handed saw, cooperating perfectly. And suddenly 'Stan' ceases to be invisible – as he is in 'everyday consciousness'. You *know* he exists, and that with his cooperation, there is almost nothing you can't do.

I have compared this to a game we used to play as children, where you stand up stiffly and fall backwards into the arms of a companion, who catches you under the armpits. But you have to trust him, and he may let you go. Stan never lets you go. This 'hidden ally' can always be trusted.

I like to tell a story of when the film producer Dino De Laurentiis asked me to London to work on the script of a horror movie. On such occasions, he would more or less lock me in an expensive hotel room, where I could order anything I liked, and pay me several thousand dollars to do radical surgery on some broken-backed script.

On one occasion, at London's Dorchester Hotel, I had ten days to rewrite one of the most muddled pieces of rubbish I've ever read. For day after day I struggled with this depressing nonsense. Finally, on the evening of the last day but one, with a third of the script still to write, I felt exhausted and utterly devoid of ideas. As I lay there on my bed, feeling on the verge of a nervous breakdown, I recalled what I had been writing just before I left Cornwall – that the right brain will never let you down. So I lay there and said, 'Come on, old right brain – for God's sake do

125

your stuff.' As soon as I'd said this, I felt an odd sense of relief, and sank into a peaceful sleep. The next morning, I woke up – still devoid of ideas – and started to work early. A single idea floated into my head and I developed it. Then another idea came ... So it went on all day, until I saw the end in sight and made a mighty effort. At five o'clock that afternoon, as Dino's secretary came to collect the pages for translation into Italian, I was writing the last sentence. I phoned Dino and asked if I could go back to Cornwall and he sent his limousine to drive me to Paddington. As we drove up Park Lane, I closed my eyes and murmured, 'Thank you, old right brain!'

Chapter Nine

A Brief Outline of History

At this point, what we urgently need is to see all this in its historical perspective. Because without such perspective, we cannot really understand what is happening *now*.

Obviously, all animals are 'right brainers'. Whitman praised the cows for not whining about their ills, but he was missing the point. Nietzsche grasped it when he said that we want to ask cows the secret of their happiness, but it's no use because they've forgotten the question before they can give the answer. The right brain *needs* the left to give it continuity and purpose.

The chief problem is a massive failure of understanding between Stan and Ollie, which produces conflict where there should be close cooperation. Once Ollie understands what produces the conflict (because he *is* the dominant one), a deep cooperation can develop that makes full use of both their resources.

Here, then, is my own 'outline of history'.

It was during the last great geological epoch, the Pleistocene (which began about one and a half million years ago) that man put on a sudden evolutionary spurt and began to outdistance all other animals. The new man, *homo habilis*, had a brain that was half as big again as his immediate predecessor, *Australopithecus*. During the next million years there emerged *homo erectus*, whose brain was twice as big as *Australopithecus*. Then, suddenly (around half a million years ago), there began what has been called 'the brain explosion'. No one knows why, but the brain of *homo erectus* expanded by another third until it reached the size of the brain of modern man – about 3 lbs. Certainly, there was no sudden social change (such as the development of tools) that would explain it. The first great 'leap forward' – hunting in bands – was millions of years old.

My own suggestion I call 'the romantic theory of evolution'. We know that, at some point, woman ceased to be 'seasonal', and became receptive to the male at all times. This was probably because if hunters were absent for weeks at a time, they expected sex when they returned home, and the women who didn't mind it produced more children, until 'seasonality' was bred out of the human species. I suspect that when hunters were away for long periods, the young men began to daydream about the girls back at home.

Sometimes, when they returned, they would find that a girl who had been quite uninteresting a few months earlier had started to develop breasts and rounded hips. Suddenly, there was reason for trying to be a mighty hunter, for the best hunters would automatically have their choice of the available women – like a modern pop star. But a great hunter requires intelligence as well as bravery. This, I would suggest, may be the cause of the 'brain explosion'. If it is true, then Goethe was right when he said, 'the eternal womanly draws us upward and on.' The brain explosion began at the same time as the last great ice age, half a million years ago, and lasted until the end of the Pleistocene, a mere 10,000 years ago. It seems likely that the periodic advance and retreat of the ice acted as a spur to man's development, forcing him to struggle harder.

Our predecessor Neanderthal Man should be mentioned here. He was around on earth between at least 300,000 and 25,000 years ago. He was regarded by many as little more than an ape-man, so it comes as a surprise to learn that the latest scientific research, revealed in the November 2006 issue of *Nature*, proves that he was very like us. His DNA was 95 per cent identical to modern humans.

Discoveries in recent years make it clear that, in certain respects, he was more intelligent than we are. He had a larger brain, and was the inventor of the bow and arrow, the blast furnace and (incredibly) superglue. This latter, a kind of pitch, was made by heating up bone to a temperature of 400 degrees in a clay furnace, and was used for securing the blade of an axe to the shaft.

He also had a religion: moon worship. In the Drachenloch cave in the Swiss Alps, a 75,000-year-old altar was discovered, along with a stone chest with a massive lid which contained bear skulls. There is a worldwide connection between the bear and the moon, and the fact that there were 13 bear skulls, the number of lunar months in the year, supports this. A perfectly circular 100,000-year-old disc, known as the Disque en Calcaire, is probably an image of the moon, which suggests a religious connection. A stone figure known as the Berekhat Ram was dismissed by many archaeologists as a natural formation until microscopic examination revealed stone dust in the grooves, proving it had been carved. Now thought to be a representation of the moon goddess, she was created a quarter of a million years ago – 220,000 years before Cro-Magnon cave paintings.

Why did Neanderthal Man vanish from earth? Probably because the slow rise in temperature that brought an end to the last ice age gradually replaced the forests that were his habitat with savannas, in which his squat build and powerful muscles ceased to be an advantage where hunting was concerned and he became, in effect, a victim of global warming. But since his brain size was about 10 per cent bigger than modern man's, he must have been at least as intelligent as we are, and probably deserves to be remembered as the true founder of civilization.

A bone discovered at Pech de L'Azé, in southern France, and dating from 200,000 years ago, contains the first-known engraving. The purpose was probably 'magical', like the cave drawings of our own ancestor Cro-Magnon man 175,000 years later – to lure animals into ambush. 200,000 years ago, man was already trying to 'control' nature. And since magic suggests some kind of religion, he had presumably developed some primitive cosmology.

Now religion is based on a sense of 'oneness with the universe', which – as we have seen – is a right-brain characteristic. So we have to see our ancestors of 200,000 years ago as already possessing 'human' intelligence – but essentially *right-brain* intelligence.

Robert Graves liked to call this kind of knowledge 'lunar

knowledge', as contrasted with the primarily left-brain knowledge of modern man, which he calls 'solar'. He himself experienced it sitting on the school roller, as already recounted (page 59): he '*knew everything*' in the sense of understanding everything. But when he tried to translate this right-brain knowledge into left-brain writing, it evaporated, leaving nothing behind.

Now you cannot create real science with right-brain intelligence, because science requires a 'storage system' for knowledge – symbols, ideas, writing. Even so, right-brain intelligence can take us a long way. Where modern man uses science, our Cro-Magnon ancestors used magic. Their 'scientists' were priests and shamans, distinguished by 'second sight' and the ability to dowse.

In my book *From Atlantis to the Sphinx*, I explain my reasons for believing that the Sphinx dates back to 10,000 BC, and was built by survivors of Atlantis. The theory arose from an observation made by an amateur Egyptologist, René Schwaller de Lubicz in the 1930s, that the Sphinx of Giza was weathered by water, not by wind-blown sand, as Egyptologists have always assumed. In 1990, Egyptologist John Anthony West invited Dr Robert Schoch, an expert on weathering, to go to Giza and examine the Sphinx, and to his delight, Schoch agreed with Schwaller de Lubicz. Wind-blown sand cuts horizontal grooves into the softer layers of rock; rain running down the face also cuts distinctive vertical grooves, and these can be clearly seen in the walls of the Sphinx enclosure. Since Egypt has had no large amounts of rain in thousands of years, it would seem that the Sphinx must be far older than 2500 BC, the date usually ascribed to it. If West and Schoch are correct, then it belongs to a far older civilization than the Egyptians who built the Great Pyramid – that of Plato's Atlantis which, Plato claims, was destroyed in a day and a night around 9600 BC. If Atlantis really existed, then it seems likely that it was the supreme example of a 'right-brain' civilization, the logical development of the culture of *homo erectus* and Cro-Magnon man.

If this, in turn, is true, then the usual view – that the Sphinx and the Great Pyramid were built by the same civilization – is as wrong as it could be. The Sphinx was a creation of a great 'lunar' civilization; the Great Pyramid – which was almost certainly built as an astronomical observatory – of one of the first 'left-brain' (solar) civilizations. Man had begun the long, slow, boring task of making catalogues and tables.

In a brilliant and convincing book, *The Origin of Consciousness in the Breakdown of the Bicameral Mind,* Julian Jaynes labels this older type of culture 'bicameral'. He believes that our primitive ancestors heard 'voices' speaking from the right brain, which they assumed to be gods. He believes that the historical evidence shows that this ancient 'oneness with the universe' began to vanish as recently as 1200 BC. He also believes that it was at this time – when man became separated from his 'other self' – that cruelty entered history. When man began to be trapped in his left brain, he began to overreact to problems with impatience and violence. It may have been the great volcanic explosion of Santorini, around 1500 BC (which destroyed a great deal of Greek civilization), that started the swing to left-brain consciousness in Europe. Soon after this, hordes of invaders known as 'the Sea Peoples' overran the Mediterranean.

Under all this stress, the old childlike mentality could no longer cope. Whatever the cause, man became increasingly cruel and destructive as his intellect developed.

A remarkable theory of the cause has been advanced in a recently published book, *The End of Eden: The Comet that Changed Civilization*, by Graham Phillips (Bear and Co, USA, 2007). He points out that in 1486 BC, the earth passed through the tail of a comet, 12P/Pons-Brooks. Until that time, many major civilizations, like that of the Hittites, the Megalithic people who built Stonehenge, the Olmecs of Mexico, the Harappans of the Indus Valley, the Jomon of Japan, and the Erlitou culture of China, had been peaceful and stable, and they now fell victim to war and mass slaughter. In the case of Harappans, the aggressors, the Aryans, had also been peaceful. Phillips's suggestion, which he admits to be without proof, is that the comet released some toxic substance, and he suggests that this could have contained the fight-or-flight hormone vasopressin, which in large doses would produce violence.

The comet is apparently due to return in 2024. We can only hope that this time the tail misses us.

However, it seems that while some men – like the Assyrians – became more cruel and violent, others – like the Greeks – developed in another direction, and began to enjoy *thinking for its own sake*. In *Symposium,* Plato shows Socrates standing on the same spot for 24 hours while he works out a problem in his head. And the dialogues of Plato reveal a man who believes that ideas are the pathway to the infinite. His mysticism is essentially a right-brain vision. But his pupil Aristotle developed in a new direction

– the observation of nature and the accumulation of facts.

It was Aristotle rather than Plato who exercised the greatest influence on the development of the western mind. The rise of the great religions – Hinduism, Buddhism, Judaism, Christianity, Islam – was of immense importance for the development of human culture. Religion provided man with a sense of order and purpose, of living in a universe he understood and in which he occupied a special place. St Augustine even objected to science on the grounds that it prevented man from focusing upon the most important thing of all – his relation to God. And in a sense, he was right. The rise of the scientific method undermined the mediaeval picture of God in heaven looking down on his creation and occasionally intervening in history.

After Copernicus and Galileo and Newton, religion went into a long, slow decline. Descartes set out to create a new kind of philosophy that began by 'doubting everything'. It was designed to place religion on a new and secure foundation; in fact, it soon exposed western man to the scepticism of David Hume, and to Kant's belief that we can never know the reality that lies behind 'phenomena'.

It was at this point, when religion seemed to have reached its lowest ebb, that a new epoch began with the publication of *Pamela*, then of Rousseau's *New Heloise*, then of Goethe's *Werther*, and man began the most interesting stage of his development so far.

Chapter Ten

Strange Powers

In the late 1960s I was asked if I would write a book about 'the occult'. I accepted because I needed the money, convinced it would turn out mostly to be self-deception and wishful thinking. But the more I learned about the subject, the more I came to recognize that 'paranormal' faculties are as well established as any other scientific 'fact'. Case after case revealed the reality of clairvoyance, telepathy and precognition.

When I realized the implications of all this I became tremendously excited. My 'Outsiders' had been saying that man is fundamentally free, and that he is a far less limited being than he thinks he is. But according to Sartre, Camus and Heidegger, man's freedom doesn't really make all that much difference to him, because he is an extraordinarily limited creature who lives in a material world that almost completely circumscribes his powers of action and swamps his ability to exercise his freedom. He is basically 'contingent' (i.e. subject to accident), and religion and belief in the supernatural are simply pathetic attempts to delude himself into thinking otherwise.

But if these cases of telepathy, clairvoyance and precognition were true, there was a whole, vast area of 'freedom' that was being overlooked by Sartre and Camus. A writer named R H Ward summarized the mystical insight in one sentence in his book, *A Drug Taker's Notes*. Describing how he had experienced it under dental gas, he wrote: '... I passed, after the first few inhalations of the gas, directly into a state of consciousness *already far more complete than the fullest degree of ordinary waking consciousness*' (my italics). Nineteenth-century Romantics had experienced these states, but had been inclined to believe they were some kind of delusion, a mere 'emotion'. Bertrand Russell tells the story of a man who experienced a kind of mystical illumination, which he wrote down; when he looked at it the next morning, it said: 'There's a strong smell of petrol around here.' On the other hand, Ouspensky, in his chapter on 'experimental mysticism', describes how, during one of his 'experiments', he thought about a trip he intended to make to Moscow that Easter, and realized clearly that he would not be able to go because certain events would arise that would make it impossible. In due course, these events arose exactly as he had foreseen them.

In his autobiography *Over the Bridge*, the poet Richard Church makes the point even more clearly. As a child he was sent to a kind of hospital to recover from an illness. One morning, he stood alone in the room, watching a gardener cut down a dead tree. Suddenly he realized that the sound of the axe did not synchronize with the blow – the sound came when the axe was on the upstroke. With a flash of intuition, Church felt that space and time are liars and fakes, and that this had suddenly been revealed to him. 'I felt both power and exultation flooding my veins ...' As a sickly child, he had always felt himself a slave of space and time, and above all, of gravity. 'Now I was free. Space and time were deceivers, openly contradicting each other ...' Church says that he realized that he 'only had to reduce them by an act of will ...' 'I exerted my will, visualising my hands and feet pressing downward on the centre of the earth. It was no surprise to me that I left the ground, and glided about the room.' He felt that he could somehow command the air to flow *through* his solid flesh. He then floated down the empty staircase to breakfast in the dining room. 'I entered and took my seat, content now to live incognito among these wingless mortals.'

Here we see how a mystical experience, similar to Ouspensky's or Bucke's, can lead to what might be called an 'anti-natural' event. There are hundreds of such cases on record. St Joseph of Copertino 'flew' repeatedly, in front of crowds of scientists (including Leibniz). Celia Greene quotes a letter sent to her describing how, as a schoolgirl, the writer lay on a table while her friends stood around chanting some rhyme, and then floated three feet off the table. I myself was once swept up into the air by Uri Geller and his friend Schipi when they merely had their index fingers under my armpits and knees (and there is a photograph to prove it).

In an early case during the 1890s, recorded by the Society for Psychical Research, a student named S M Beard was reading a book on the power of the will when he suddenly decided to try to 'appear' to his girlfriend Miss Verity. As he made an effort, he suddenly felt 'frozen', unable to move his limbs. At that moment, Miss Verity awoke, to find him standing by her bed; she shrieked and her 11-year-old sister also woke up and saw him. Beard then vanished.

Beard later did it a second time, putting forth 'an effort which I cannot find words to describe. I was aware of a mysterious influence permeating my body, *and had a distinct impression that I was exercising some force with which I had hitherto been unacquainted, but which I can now at certain times set in motion at will.'* He then 'appeared' again to Miss Verity's sister. In neither case was Beard aware of what was happening – as far as he was concerned, he was in a trance back in his room. But the Verities confirmed it to the Society for Psychical Research.

Note that Beard had been reading a book on the power of the will, and was therefore experiencing a sense of 'potentiality' – as Bucke did after an evening studying Shelley and Whitman.

My friend Mark Bredin, a pianist, was being driven home in a taxi along the Bayswater Road, after a concert – very relaxed – when he *knew* that, at the Queensway traffic lights, another taxi would try to jump the light and hit their taxi side-on. It happened moments later, exactly as he had foreseen it.

Now we can probably explain telepathy and clairvoyance in terms of some unknown power of the right brain – the novelist Upton Sinclair called it 'mental radio'. But explaining precognition quite simply demands that we accept that we are profoundly mistaken in our view of ourselves as creatures confined in space and time. Time, like everyday consciousness, seems to be a liar. What is the alternative? It would seem that, in some way, we exist *outside* space and time. The 'real' world is not at all like the world our senses – and our assumptions – reveal to us. In the 'real' world, we possess powers that we do not even suspect. But we need to make an *effort* to free ourselves from the habitual assumptions of the robot.

No subject makes this more clear than synchronicity. Really *preposterous* coincidences give us a strong sense that what we assume to be 'reality' is really some kind of deception. Jung liked to recount the extraordinary case of M de Fortgibu told by poet Emile Deschamps. As a child in Orleans, Deschamps tasted plum pudding for the first time in the company of M de Fortgibu, who had recently returned from England. Ten years later, passing a restaurant, he saw plum pudding for the first time since that day. When he asked for a slice, they told him it was reserved for another gentleman, who turned out to be M de Fortgibu – now an elderly gentleman. M de Fortgibu happily shared it with Deschamps. Years later, invited to dinner, Deschamps was offered plum pudding, and proceeded to tell his hosts the Fortgibu story. As he did so, M de Fortgibu – now very old and rather confused – walked into the room. He had been invited to dinner in another flat, and had mistaken the door.

When writing an article about synchronicity (for *An Encyclopedia of Unsolved Mysteries*), I began to experience a series of absurd synchronicities, the oddest of which was as follows. I was describing an experience of the 'Ufologist' Jacques Vallee, who became interested in a Los Angeles religious cult known as the Order of Melchizedec – Melchizedek being one of the more obscure biblical prophets. Vallee had searched for information about the prophet, but without much success.

In the midst of this search, he took a taxi, and asked his lady taxi driver for a receipt. She gave him a receipt signed 'M Melchizedec'. He thought this an amusing coincidence, which suggested that there were more Melchizedecs around than he had assumed. But when he checked the Los Angeles telephone directory – a vast compilation in several volumes – he found only one Melchizedec – his taxi driver.

Vallee said it was as if he had stuck a notice on some universal notice board: 'Wanted – Melchizedecs', and some earnest guardian angel had asked: 'How about this?' 'No, no, that's no good – that's a taxi driver.'

Vallee goes on to point out that there are two ways in which a librarian can store information. One is in alphabetical order. But a simpler system would be to place each book on the nearest shelf as it arrives, and have some straightforward method of retrieving it – like a 'beeper' on the spine of every book, which would respond to a radio signal by making a noise to signal its position. Vallee is suggesting that this may be how the universe is con-structed – on a system known as a 'random data base' – and that it could explain apparent synchronicities.

After I had finished writing about Vallee's synchronicity, I broke off my day's work to take my dogs for a walk. As I was leaving my work room, I noticed on the camp bed a book that had obviously fallen off the shelf, and which I did not recognize. It was called *You Are Sentenced to Life*, by Dr W D Chesney, and I had obviously bought it many years before in California and sent it for binding. But I had never actually read it. When I came back from my walk, I glanced through the book – and discovered, at the very end, a page headed 'ORDER OF MELCHIZEDEC'. It was a letter to the author from the founder of the Order, Grace Hooper Pettipher.

I had cited Vallee's story about Melchizedec as one of the most preposterous synchronicities I know. Finding yet another reference to the Order within an hour or so of writing about it – I have about 30,000 books in my house – obviously involved a coincidence that would be beyond numerical calculation. It was as if the 'guardian angel' had said, 'You think that's preposterous? Well how about this?'

It was shortly after this that, reading some text about Hermes Trismegistus, the legendary founder of magic, and his famous formula 'as above, so below' (which is supposed to express the essence of magic), I felt for the first time that I understood the inner meaning of the saying. It is generally taken to refer to the magical system of 'correspondences', the idea that earthly things have a heavenly connection. (For example, the days of the weeks are named after gods, and a magician who wished to perform a ceremony to ensure wealth would choose Sunday as the best day, since the sun is associated with gold.) What suddenly struck me is that we are all accustomed to the fact that the environment can act upon the mind, so that a dull day can make us depressed, and so on. But the fundamental tenet of 'occultism' (and the basic assertion of this book) is that the mind possesses hidden powers that can influence the external world. This seems to happen by a process of 'induction', not unlike that involved in a simple electrical transformer. If, for example, I wish to use my British electric razor when I am in America, I have to buy a transformer which will 'step-up'

American voltage (120) to British voltage (240). If I want to use an American razor in England, I have to reverse the same trans-former (which merely involves connecting it up back-to-front) to step-down 240 volts to 120.

Like most people, I have often observed that when I am in an optimistic and purposeful state, things tend to 'go right'. When I am tired and depressed, they go wrong – as if I have wired-up my 'mind transformer' the wrong way round, so it causes 'lower' vibrations in the external world. Optimism, on the other hand, seems to induce more powerful vibrations in the external world, and these in turn induce 'serendipity' – a term coined by Horace Walpole, meaning 'the faculty of making happy and unexpected discoveries by chance.'

Another personal example. On Saturday evenings I made a habit of spending an hour in the local pub, meeting friends, drinking wine and eating sandwiches. One evening, driving home from the pub, I began talking to my wife Joy about how we take for granted all kinds of 'conveniences' – for example, that our car will get us home without problems. As I spoke, the car went slower and slower, then stopped. The problem was not too serious, and Joy got a lift home and returned with the Land Rover. She forgot the tow-rope, but fortunately there proved to be one in the boot of the car, and we got home without trouble, hardly even late. The garage that looked at the car said it had developed a rare – but easily corrected – electrical fault that they had never encountered before. It was as if, once again, the god of synchronicity overheard me, and set out to show me that life is not really governed by the laws of chance.

Now, although it was Jung who coined the word synchronicity (in collaboration with the physicist Wolfgang Pauli) in 1950, he did not invent it. For this, the credit must go to the Viennese biologist Paul Kammerer, who was fascinated by coincidence and began collecting examples at the age of 20 (in 1900). A typical one concerned two young soldiers called Franz Richter, both admitted to the same military hospital with pneumonia. Both were 19, born in Silesia, and volunteers in the Transport Corps. He collected a hundred such coincidences in his book *The Law of Seriality* (*Das Gesetez der Serie*) in 1919. As the title implies, he did not believe that coincidence is a matter of chance, but that there is some unidentified principle in the universe that draws like together, a kind of gravitational force concerning events. If coincidence piles on coincidence he called it a progressive series, as in the following case:

> On July 28, 1915, I experienced the following
> progressive series: (a) my wife was reading about
> 'Mrs. Rohan', a character in the novel *Michael* by
> Hermann Bang; in the tramway she saw a man who
> looked like her friend, Prince Josef Rohan; in the
> evening Prince Rohan dropped in on us; (b) In the
> tram she overheard somebody asking the pseudo-
> Rohan whether he knew the village of Weissenbach
> on Lake Attersee, and whether it would be a pleasant
> place for a holiday. When she got out of the tram,
> she went to a delicatessen shop on the Naschmarkt,
> where the attendant asked her whether she

happened to know Weissenbach on Lake Attersee –
he had to make a delivery by mail and did not know
the correct postal address.

Jung cites many such examples in his essay *Synchronicity – An A-causal Connecting Principle*. The title is, of course, meaningless, suggesting a causal principle that is not causal. His notion differs from Kammerer's in that he is not suggesting some scientific 'law', but believes that the unconscious mind is responsible. For example, he tells how he was having considerable difficulty with a young female patient 'who always knew better about everything' and whose rationalism seemed impregnable. One day, as she was telling Jung about a vivid dream of a golden scarab, there was a tapping on the window: Jung opened it and a gold-green scarab – a rose-chafer – flew into the room. Jung caught it and handed it to the patient. 'Here is your scarab.' This 'punctured the desired hole in her rationalism' and broke the ice of her resistance.

Although Jung's collaboration with Pauli was not until 1950 he had, in fact, been concerned with 'synchronicity' since 1920, when he began to make use of the *I Ching*, or *Book of Changes*. He kept silent about this, obviously afraid of being regarded as a crank. But in 1943, at the age of 68, he slipped on an icy road and broke his ankle, as a result of which he suffered a severe heart attack, and while in hospital had several 'near-death' visions, such as seeing the earth from outer space. These seem to have convinced him of the importance of frankness about his interest in the paranormal, and led him to give a lecture on synchronicity at the Eranos Conference in 1951. As he expected, it caused many psychologists to suspect that his brain was softening with old age. But the immense increase in his reputation in his later years, when he came to be regarded as a universal guru, demonstrates that an increasing number of admirers did not share this view.

As far as I am concerned, the implication of synchronicity would seem to be that when we are in spiritual health, so to speak, with a high level of vital purpose and making use of our freedom, synchronicities tend to favour us. This also implies clearly that gloom and depression are dangerous states of mind, and explains why I react so strongly against pessimists like Beckett, whom I regard as a polluter of the wellsprings of our culture. In *The Outsider* I suggested that the lesson of Camus's *L'Etranger* and Kafka's *Metamorphosis* is that if you cease to make all effort, fate takes advantage of this lowering of your spiritual guard by hitting you on the head. Camus himself continued to believe that life is maliciously absurd, rather like Thomas Hardy, and he died in his forties in a stupid car accident.

In short, human beings *do* possess freedom, but most of the time they waste it by living 'robotically'. Yet we only have to make an effort to raise our vitality by one degree, so we are 49 per cent robot and 51 per cent 'real you', to recognize that freedom is a reality.

A girl I know was in a state of anguish because her husband was being unfaithful, and decided to leave him to keep house for her brother, an academic, in Oregon. Her husband, another academic, promised to mend his ways and begged her to move with him to a new job in Ohio. For days she agonized: 'Oregon or

Ohio?' until one night, as she lay awake, it hit her like a thunder-bolt: 'I don't have to go to Oregon or Ohio. *I'm free.*' She said that for days afterwards she walked around on air – even her tennis improved. The recognition of freedom is another name for 'power consciousness'.

She was *driven* to perception of freedom by 'suffering'. But according to Gurdjieff, we can achieve it deliberately by 'intentional suffering' – that is, by effort of will. And once we move into this realm of 'freedom', the most astonishing things begin to happen.

Chapter Eleven

Faculty X and the Sexual Vision

In *The Occult* I coined the term 'Faculty X' to pin down the odd ability to grasp the *reality* of some other time and place. It is basically 'duo-consciousness', being in two places at once. The most typical example we have considered is in *Swann's Way*, the *moment bienheureux* triggered by the madeleine. For a split second, Marcel *became* the child who lived in Combray. Before tasting the cake, Proust's hero could have said, 'I was a child who lived in Combray.' Now he can say it and *mean* it. It is as if he has suddenly acquitted another dimension – a time dimension. We can also see that the BBC producer who 'became' Schubert was experiencing a form of Faculty X (page 5).

Marcel's experience relates to Proust's own past. In *A Study of History*, Arnold Toynbee describes a number of flashes of Faculty X that related to the historical past. The idea of the book came to him when he climbed Mount Taygetus, in Sparta, and was sitting in the citadel of Mistra; the city had been a ruin ever since it was destroyed by the Turks in 1821. As, in a state of deep relaxation, he looked at a broken wall, it was suddenly as if he could *see* the invaders pouring through the gap. Time had disappeared. It was not some hallucination – the destruction of Mistra simply became as real as if it was happening *now*.

He goes on to describe half a dozen more occasions when the past had suddenly 'come to life'. The most interesting happened as he was passing Victoria Station during World War I, and had a momentary insight into *all* history, like some great river, in which his own life was a tiny wavelet.

Now there are some respects in which these moments of Faculty X resemble those odd psychic occurrences known as 'time slips', moments in which people glimpse some past event. One of the most famous of these occurred to two English ladies, Miss Moberley and Miss Jourdain, at Versailles in 1911, when they apparently found themselves back in the Trianon of Louis XVI and Marie Antoinette. (There is a general impression that this story has been 'disproved', but this is quite untrue.)

Similarly, in *Mysteries*, I have recorded a detailed account by a friend, Jane O'Neill, of how she visited the church in Fotheringhay, and somehow saw it as it was in the time of Mary Queen of Scots. She had been involved in an appalling accident not long before, and was still in a shattered state – these odd faculties often seem to develop after shocks or traumas.

Now 'time slips' are baffling enough. But Toynbee's many experiences do not quite involve time slips – even though he records that when they happen, he has an odd sensation like an aeroplane lurching as it falls into an air pocket – he called them 'time pockets'. After all, he *knew* what had happened at Mistra, because he was a historian. On another occasion, Toynbee was looking at the site of the battle of Pharsalus when he slipped into a 'time pocket'. A heavy mist seemed to come down (as it actually had before the battle), after which he saw the battle, and averted his eyes at the massacre of the Greeks. As he did so he caught sight of fleeing horsemen, of whose identity he was ignorant. (The ideal sequel would be that he later checked his history books and learned the identity of the horsemen – unfortunately, this didn't happen – but the unidentified horsemen emphasize the real quality of what he saw.)

What appears to have happened is that Toynbee's *knowledge* of history seems to have entered into some kind of combination with some odd faculty of deep relaxation, producing these 'visions'.

What I am suggesting is that we can generate Faculty X through the deliberate exercise of 'imagination' – not imagination in the usual sense of mere fantasy, but in Blake's sense of conjuring up another reality. A historian like Toynbee must have spent a great deal of his time at famous historical sites, trying to conjure up what happened. And this exercise of imagination must have prepared the ground for his moments of Faculty X.

The playwright August Strindberg had a similar experience. He was sitting in a café, trying to persuade a friend not to undertake a certain course of action. He was reminding him of a previous occasion when they had had a similar discussion, in the Augustiner Tavern. As he conjured up the scene, Strindberg suddenly found himself *in* the Augustiner Tavern, with total strangers entering the door. His friend was terrified at the sudden blank look on his face, 'as if he had died'. Now what Strindberg *should* have done was to rush to the Augustiner Tavern and see if the strangers were in there. He didn't. But another occasion seems to suggest that the experience was real, and not a hallucination. In Paris, alone, he found himself feeling a deep, nostalgic longing for the home of his wife in Bavaria. As he 'imagined' this, he seemed to be in the drawing room, with his mother-in-law playing the piano. Suddenly, she looked up and stared at him in amazement, and his 'image' disappeared. Soon after he received a letter from her asking: 'Are you well? I was playing the piano when I looked up and saw you standing there.'

Clearly, this is also related to 'projections' like Beard's 'appearance' to Miss Verity. It may also be related to an experience described by Ouspensky during his 'mystical' experiments; he says that, after one of these, his sense of reality was so amplified that as he walked in the street he could see *every detail* of the faces of people who were too far away to be anything but a blur under normal circumstances. This may suggest that his sight became abnormally strong. Or it may be that *some other faculty*, apart from sight, was involved.

Faculty X is obviously a sudden sense of *power over time*. In *The Occult* I describe how I once achieved it by an effort of will. At that time (in my early twenties) I was studying Nijinsky's choreography for the *Rite of Spring*, with its stiff, hieratic movements. One day in my room, I was listening to the liebestod from *Tristan and Isolde,* and stood up and began to perform 'Nijinsky movements' to the music.

At the height of the climax, I achieved such an intensity of concentration that I had a clear sense of being above – or beyond –

time. To be more precise, I recognized time as a process associated with my body. When we are tired and dull, time drags; when we are excited and happy, it flashes past. But even when most happy, we feel enslaved by time. In this moment, I felt as if I had *halted* time. All this confirms my feeling that the real problem of human beings is that the will is too feeble – we are like grandfather clocks driven by watch springs, or like a huge millwheel driven by a muddy trickle of water. And this is because we make the mistake of regarding ourselves as basically passive. A passive person gradually stagnates – or rather, his mental flow is blocked up by a kind of sedimentation. We need to maintain enough recognition of the active nature of consciousness to prevent this occurring.

Also relevant to this discussion are the comments I made in chapter five about William Blake and Count Ludwig von Zinzendorf (page 74). In 1750, Zinzendorf was the organizer of a Moravian church in Fetter Lane, London, whose pastor was Zinzendorf's disciple Peter Boehler. The congregation included the mystic Emmanuel Swedenborg, who had developed his own form of sexual/religious mysticism. Zinzendorf had already concluded that sex could be used to intensify religious vision, and had taught an inner circle among his followers to make use of sexual excitement to create a state of ecstasy that could last all night. William Blake's mother and father were amongst those who practised it.

What Zinzendorf was out to induce was undoubtedly a form of Faculty X – sex deliberately amplified by the imagination, in the way that a fire can be made to crackle into flame from a few sparks – which might be conveniently labelled the 'Sexual Vision'. The prelude to such intensity is commonly a build-up of frustration, something Blake understood very well:

> The moment of desire! the moment of
> desire! The virgin
> That pines for man shall awaken her womb
> to enormous joys
> In the secret shadows of her chamber: the
> youth shut up from
> The lustful joy shall forget to generate, and
> create an amorous image
> In the shadows of his curtains and in the
> folds of his silent pillow ...

'The Visions of the Daughters of Albion'

Yet obviously, sheer determined concentration could be just as effective. The reason few achieve the intensity of the 'Sexual Vision' is obvious: we lose focus too easily; the 'robot' takes over. Sex, after all, depends upon a feeling of 'strangeness', even an element of forbiddenness, between the couple. And this is induced more easily when there is a distance between them than in when they are in direct physical contact in bed. This is why a male is likely to achieve enormous intensity of desire when he catches an unexpected glimpse of a woman taking off her clothes. Compared to this shock, the pleasure generated by two bodies pressed together – in which the visual element is restricted – is bound to be diluted.

Zinzendorf made deliberate use of the amplification technique in his sexual/religious mysticism. Martha Schuchard writes: 'For Swedenborg, Kabbalists and Tantrists, this shared psychoerotic state could only be achieved if the male mastered the meditation process that creates "continual potency" – a prolonged erection which arrested or delayed ejaculation,' and adds that Swedenborg (like Zinzendorf) 'argues that control and prolongation of the male erection is crucial to the visionary state'.

But of course, an erection is not maintained by 'meditation', but by sexual imagination. What can happen then is a kind of feedback process of excitement that leads to 'Sexual Vision' in which excitement feeds off itself and, provided it is not terminated by orgasm, can be maintained in a state of balance for minutes or hours. To understand the mechanism of this process we only have to recall William James's comment in 'A Suggestion About Mysticism': 'What happened each time was that I seemed all at once to be reminded of a past experience; and this reminiscence, ere I could conceive or name it distinctly, developed into something further that belonged with it, this in turn into something further still, and so on, until the process faded out, leaving me amazed at the sudden vision of increasing ranges of distant facts.' In essence, the 'Sexual Vision' is, like this, associative.

The truth is that all healthy people have a fairly strong sexual imagination. The evidence of his poetry indicates that Blake's was exceptionally active. So when, at the age of 25, he married 17-year-old Catherine Boucher, he was undoubtedly long-acquainted with the daydreams created 'in the shadow of his curtains and the folds of his silent pillow'. By that time, Count Zinzendorf had been dead for 25 years, otherwise Blake would certainly have been delighted to become a member of the congregation of the sexual guru of his mother and father.

And what of the claim that the essence of the visionary state consisted in maintaining an erection for hours at a time?

That sounds impossible, but it would be premature to dismiss it. In 1989 I wrote a book called *The Misfits*, in which a great deal of space was devoted to the sexual theories of the late Charlotte Bach. She believed that sexuality depends on a complex balance between the male and female elements in the psyche, and had been convinced by a practitioner of the method that an orgasm could be sustained indefinitely – this man claimed to have experienced an eight-hour orgasm. She believed that through the practice of a kind of sexual yoga, the glow of sexuality could be maintained almost indefinitely, just as an electric bulb can burn for hundreds of hours without burning out.

And obviously, since the invention of viagra, the body has had a chemical ally to facilitate the Sexual Vision.

Now an important philosophical question arises from all this: is sexual vision basically some kind of illusion? This amounts, of course, to a basic problem of human perception. A view from a mountaintop is more satisfying to our aesthetic sense than a view from the valley, for 'close-upness deprives us of meaning'. This does not mean that, because a view loses half its charm when we get close to it, we dismiss the beauty we perceived from a distance as an illusion. We simply accept it as another case of 'the near and the far', and the fact that the 'promise of the horizon' is always beyond our reach.

With sex, the case is different. Philosophers have always been suspicious of sexual beauty, because they regard it as a lure whose purpose is the continuation of the species. After all, the beauty of the face that launched a thousand ships is only skin-deep. No wonder Cupid is seen as a mischievous child who fires arrows tipped with a poison that induces hallucinations.

But both Zinzendorf and Blake would certainly have dismissed this negative view. Zinzendorf would have pointed out, rightly, that an excitement that can be maintained throughout a whole night must be based upon perception of reality. And here Maslow might be called as a witness. As an example of the peak experience, he cited a marine who had been on a Pacific island for years without seeing a woman and who, when he came back to base and saw a nurse, had a strong peak experience, because *he suddenly realized that women are different from men, as different as horses are from cows.* In other words, his long abstinence from the opposite sex made him see women quite objectively, as if they were an unknown species. His reaction to the question of whether sex is an illusion would have been a derisive laugh.

We may take it, therefore that the 'Sexual Vision' is an authentic form of Faculty X.

Chapter Twelve

Philosophy

This book has been constructed rather like one of the seminars I used to give in the 1960s at the Esalen Institute at Big Sur, near San Francisco – an attempt to draw in the readers with a practical sense of what can be done through mental disciplines. But I usually insisted that we devote one session to making a real intellectual effort to grasp this in terms of western philosophy. Oddly enough, many students seemed to find this one of the most rewarding sessions.

In my book *Beyond the Outsider* (1965) there is a chapter called 'The Strange Story of Modern Philosophy', and in what follows, I shall recapitulate its arguments.

I begin by considering the 'world rejection' of Socrates, who tells his followers that since the philosopher spends his life trying to separate his soul from his body, his own death should be regarded as a consummation. This is consistent with his questionable belief that only spirit is real, and matter is somehow unimportant and unreal. The notion would persist throughout the next 2,000 years, harmonizing comfortably with the Christian view that this world is unimportant compared to the next. It may be needless to say that I totally reject it.

Then came scientific thought, in the person of Galileo Galilei, who introduced the spirit of experiment. He demonstrated that gravity makes all bodies fall at the same speed, and 'invented' the telescope through which he discovered the moons of Jupiter. From then on, human thought began to take a more purposeful direction. In 1642, the year Galileo died, Newton was born, and within 40 years, science had advanced further than in the previous 2,000.

In philosophy, a similar leap forward had taken place while Galileo was still alive. René Descartes attempted to bring into philosophy the same kind of certainty that Galileo had brought to science. Galileo had explored the heavens with a telescope; Descartes decided to examine the human situation through a kind of magnifying glass. His aim was to ask what we can really know for certain.

His new method of achieving certainty was simplicity itself: *to doubt everything*. After seeing some toy robots driven by water in the park at Versailles, it struck him that human beings are almost entirely mechanical; we need stimuli to make us do something. Of course, men could not be made of clockwork, because they have souls. (Descartes was a good Catholic.) But animals could be, and probably are, machines.

How do I know I am not a machine? Because a machine has no self-awareness. On the other hand, I can think, 'therefore I am'. Such an assertion obviously leaves room for doubt. If some god could endow a washing machine with self-awareness, it would probably assume that it operates of its own free will, and might well say, 'I think, therefore I am.' It would clearly be mistaken.

The British philosopher John Locke – who was 18 when Descartes died – recognized this. He did not actually argue that men are robots, but came very close to it when he said that we cannot know anything that does not come from our experience. There is nothing in the mind that was not first in the senses. When man is born, his mind is like a blank sheet of paper, a '*tabula rasa*'. Everything he then learns arises from things that happen to him. So what we call the mind – all our thoughts, responses, reactions – is a 'construct', like a house built of pieces of Lego.

Descartes had launched modern western philosophy with a dubious proposition, and now Locke continued it with an even more dubious one. This seems to be a typical characteristic of western philosophy: if someone makes a stupid howler, his successors try to justify it and carry the thing to even further lengths of absurdity, when common sense would suggest that they get their foundations right by going back to square one.

So it was perhaps inevitable that Bishop Berkeley should go a step further. If we can only know things through the mind, then why should we assume the outside world exists at all? Jam is not really sweet; it only produces a sensation of sweetness on the tongue. The sky is not really blue; it only produces a sense of blueness on the eyes. Perhaps objects only exist when we are looking at them, and when there is no one there to see them, they vanish. Or at least, they would if God was not there to see them.

This was obviously inviting some clever trouble-maker to suggest that, since there is no evidence that God exists, perhaps everything is an illusion? Which is more or less what the next 'great philosopher' did by carrying doubt even further. David Hume set out to reduce everything to materialism. The soul, which Descartes thought he had proved, is an illusion, because when I look inside myself, I do not become aware of 'the essential me', but merely of thoughts and sensations. So human beings are also made of Lego.

And when you look at things in this piecemeal way, they simply dissolve. Even cause and effect are seen to be an illusion, for 'every effect is a distinct event from its cause', and therefore 'cannot be discovered in the cause'. Perhaps God is pulling our legs when He makes a kettle boil on a fire; perhaps it is really supposed to freeze.

What Hume did was to sweep the world bare of all certainty, leaving philosophy looking like a landscape after the dropping of an H-bomb. In fact, his Scottish contemporary Thomas Reid had seen through the fallacy that underlay Hume's philosophy.

According to Hume, when we open our eyes in the morning, we do not see 'things' but 'ideas' (or 'impressions'). That object by the side of my bed is a clock, but if I had never seen or heard of a clock, I wouldn't know this. Before I can grasp what I am looking at I need to know what a clock is – and that is an idea. And the same goes for everything else – that door, window, chest of drawers.

Hume believed that ideas are simply faded impressions of sense. If he thought of Edinburgh Castle, what came into his head was something like a faded picture of Edinburgh Castle. So all we can really know is a faded universe of impressions inside our heads.

Now Reid was much influenced by his professor George Turnbull, who argued that our common-sense view of facts, such as that the external world exists, cannot be overturned by reasoning, and that philosophy should be based on our 'active power', the power of the will. So Reid could not accept that all our knowledge is based on mere ideas and impressions. I may believe this when I have spent the day writing and thinking, but that is because too much thinking makes things seem less real; but the moment I step outdoors and encounter the sun and the wind, I know better.

Now anyone who has read Aldous Huxley's book *The Doors of Perception* will recognize what he means. What startled Huxley after he had taken mescalin was the realization that everything is ten times as real as he thought. Millions of students in the 1960s experienced the same revelation when they took mescalin or LSD: that the world 'out there' is seething with pure existence. And if Hume had taken mescalin he would have recognized immediately that his belief that ideas are faded impressions of sense is simply untrue.

But Reid was not influential enough to counterbalance Locke, Berkeley and Hume and the doubts they had instilled, let alone Descartes.

The philosopher who tried to repair the damage was the Königsburg professor Immanuel Kant. And what he did was, in effect, to take a step backward to Bishop Berkeley, and make the mind the creator of reality.

He noticed the existence of what Husserl would later call 'intentionality' – that the mind makes sense of this chaotic world that surrounds us by imposing order on it. We divide things into categories – for example, everything I can see around me is either a liquid, a solid or a gas. We use clocks to impose order on the chaos of time, and measuring rods to impose it on space. We call things by words we have invented – that four-legged creature is a 'cat', and that one a 'dog'. You could say we invent space and time to make our world orderly enough to live in comfortably. It is as if we had invented a pair of spectacles that impose categories on the world.

Does that mean there is no 'true reality' behind all our categories? Yes, there *is* such an underlying reality, which Kant called the noumenon, to distinguish it from the world of mere 'phenomena' that surrounds us. *But since we can never remove the spectacles, we can never know this reality.*

The dramatist Heinrich von Kleist was so upset by Kant's bewildering variation on Bishop Berkeley that he committed suicide. At which point one of Kant's followers, a now almost forgotten thinker called Johann Gottlieb Fichte, called a halt to the madness – at least, he would have done if anyone had taken any notice of him. What Fichte said was: why bother about this 'noumenon'? If it is unknowable, we may as well forget it. In that case, man is left in a world created by his senses – just as Berkeley said. But if 'I' really created the universe, why do I not know that I did? There must be two 'me's', this everyday self who has no idea of what is going on, and another 'me' who is actually a kind of god who has created this world.

Descartes had sat in his armchair, or more likely lay in bed (he was notoriously lazy) and asked: 'What can I know for certain?'

He answered: 'Two things are certain – my own existence and that world out there.' We call them the subjective and the objective worlds. Fichte said: 'No, there are three worlds – that world out there, and two "me's", the ordinary me and the me who is behind the scenes creating the world out there.'

The next question is: how could the ordinary 'me' begin to explore the extraordinary world created by the 'other me'? And this, of course, is the true task of phenomenology, to which we shall come in a moment.

Fichte made one more comment that is of immense importance: that the trouble with philosophy was that its attitude to the world is passive. But philosophy, he said (in *Addresses to the German Nation*), should regard itself as active, or at least as a prelude to action. This, of course, is very close to George Turnbull's common sense and his belief in the 'active power'.

Expressed in this way, this sounds unexciting – as if it is merely an earlier statement of Karl Marx's remark that the business of philosophy is not to understand the world but to change it. In fact, it was really a blinding flash of insight: that Kantian philosophy turned philosophers into armchair theorists, so that their whole attitude to knowledge was passive, when to really grasp reality it should be active.

As Buckminster Fuller once expressed it: 'I seem to be a verb.'

As to that other problem, that philosophical hare set running by Descartes, the solution seems to lie in Fichte's insight that we have 'two selves'. Descartes should have followed up his assertion 'I think therefore I am' with the question: 'Yes, but who am I?' He is failing to question his own identity, and this error will lead on to the errors of Locke, Berkeley, Hume, Kant, Hegel and the rest.

By the beginning of the 19th century, philosophy had fallen into a sad state. For the doubts planted by Locke, Berkeley and Hume had made the philosopher see himself as essentially passive – someone who sat in an armchair, asking what his reason could tell him about the world. Even as early as 1744, this attitude had led one French philosopher, Julien Offray de la Mettrie, to write a book called *Man the Machine*, suggesting that is all we really are.

We need not get too irritated by this, for la Mettrie's intention was not to convince us that life is meaningless, but to annoy the Church, which had exercised a stranglehold on freedom of thought for centuries. (He succeeded all too well, and after being dismissed from the army on the complaint of the chaplain, he was then forced to flee Leiden by angry theologians; fortunately Frederick the Great then offered him refuge in Prussia.) In most of Europe, Protestantism had taken hold, reducing the power of the Church to put heretics in jail, but in France, Italy and Spain, heretics could still be tried and imprisoned.

La Mettrie was followed by Etienne de Condillac and Pierre Cabanis. Condillac argued that our so-called mental life is merely a matter of physical sensations, and Cabanis, a doctor, that the brain secretes thoughts as the liver secretes bile. Just as the stomach and intestines receive food and digest it, so the brain receives impressions, digests them, and the result is thought.

Now Condillac and Cabanis were members of a group known as 'Les Philosophes', which might today be translated as 'the intellectuals'. A younger member of this group was an aristocrat called Maine de Biran, a soldier who retired to a castle in the

Dordogne to devote his life to philosophy. Although he started off as a follower of Condillac, he gradually became more and more opposed to this idea that man is nothing more than a kind of penny-in-the-slot machine. His objection runs along these lines: when I am making a real effort, I have a clear feeling that it is I who am doing it, not a machine. I may feel mechanical when I'm doing something boring and automatic, but as soon as I exert my will, I become aware that I'm not a machine – that I possess an 'active power'.

This vital insight could have altered the course of French philosophy, but no one was interested in pursuing the notion that man possesses free will. Frenchmen at the end of the 18th century were so intoxicated at being able to give a two-finger salute to the Catholic Church – which had persecuted free thought for centuries – that they had no intention of conceding that man had an immortal soul. So no one paid the slightest attention to Maine de Biran's discovery that we have free will. The next major French philosopher, Auguste Comte, directed all his polemical powers at denouncing superstition (by which he meant religion), and declaring that man would never be free until he learned to live by logic and reason alone. He also regarded metaphysics –i.e. all attempts to deal with larger questions about man and the universe – as another form of superstition. Unfortunately, he was a poor advertisement for his religion of reason, for a disastrous marriage caused a nervous breakdown that drove him into an insane asylum, after which an unhappy love affair made him attempt suicide. In spite of this, his *Course of Positive Philosophy* had an enormous influence, and he even founded a 'Church of Humanity', which went on to become highly successful after his death.

In Germany, metaphysical philosophy showed that it still had plenty of life in it in the thought of G F Hegel, who also began as a sceptic and a rationalist, but then had some kind of revelation in which he saw the 'Idea' as the ultimate reality from which all other things derive, including Nature and Spirit.

Perhaps he was remembering St John's 'In the beginning was the Word.' This led him to a vision of history that has something in common with Toynbee's, in which all the miseries and torments of history nevertheless drive man 'upward and on', towards the expression of pure spirit. There was something very vital and positive about Hegel's philosophy that aroused immense enthusiasm in his contemporaries, and led to a revival of interest in metaphysics. At a time when the world was almost ready to surrender to French materialism, it was Hegel who brought a refreshing new impulse of Idealism. If it had not been for his tendency to write in incomprehensible abstractions, he would probably qualify as the most important philosopher since Plato.

The man who now seems to us to be one of the most original thinkers of the mid-19th century was totally unknown in his own time. Søren Kierkegaard, a brilliant but intensely neurotic Dane, might have been expected to regard Hegel as a fellow-spirit, since neither had the slightest inclination towards what the French called positivism. But studying Hegel at Copenhagen University put him off completely, since he felt this was all too abstract, and therefore had little to say to him as an individual. As a result, he developed an intense dislike of this philosopher who claimed to have answered every major question in the universe.

It was Kierkegaard who first used the word existential (to mean the opposite of 'abstract') to explain his dislike of Hegel. When books like *The Concept of Angst* were rediscovered in the 1920s, they immediately found a large audience, because by that time everybody was suffering from it. Probably his best known statement is: 'Truth is subjectivity'.

Kierkegaard spent most of his short life (he died at the age of 42) in a state of depression, and collapsed on the day he went to withdraw the last of his money from the bank. In this sense he was typical of the Romantics who, ever since Rousseau, had been complaining that they found life too difficult and unrewarding to be worth the effort. And this is why Fichte's insight that there is a part of the mind that creates the world 'behind our backs' is so important. It suggested that if poets and philosophers knew enough about the hidden powers of that 'other self', they might find life less intolerable.

As to French philosophy, its mainstream remained as materialistic as ever. The man who was basically responsible for this was the father of scepticism, David Hume.

We have already noted Thomas Reid's attempt to demonstrate that Hume's philosophy was based on a fallacy: namely, that all our knowledge is based on ideas or impressions. But in the 20th century, a far more considerable thinker than Reid set out to refute Hume. His name was Alfred North Whitehead.

As we have seen, Hume argued that we have no true 'inner self'. He claimed that when he looked inside himself for 'the real David Hume', he only came across ideas and impressions, but nothing like a 'self'. And he concluded that all that can be found inside us is a 'stream of consciousness', a lot of scurrying thoughts whose only 'identity' is that they come one after another. This is the realization that comes, he says, when you look at your inner self through a magnifying glass.

In a little book called *Symbolism, Its Meaning and Effect*, Whitehead points out that this method of looking at something through a magnifying glass is a good way of missing its meaning. If, for example, you looked at a great painting through a magnifying glass, you would only see the texture of the paint. If you look at a newspaper photograph close up, you would only see disconnected dots. In both cases you are looking at individual trees and failing to see that they constitute a wood. In order to see the wood, we need to take a bird's-eye view, to stand back.

So we have two kinds of perception: bird's-eye and worm's-eye; far-off and close-up. Both only give half the picture.

Whitehead calls these two modes 'presentational immediacy' and 'causal efficacy'. The first is easy to understand – what is in front of your nose. The second is more difficult. The example Whitehead gives is the words 'United States'. You do not grasp these piecemeal: 'United – that means held together. States – yes, that means states like Florida and California. Oh yes, that means America.' You see the two words as one, Unitedstates, and register that as 'America'. Cause and effect blend into one.

Now Hume criticized causality by saying that every effect is quite distinct from its cause, and so is not 'necessarily' linked to it. Whitehead replies: When you grasp a 'meaning', cause and effect are not merely 'linked – they are one.

We might say, then, that we have two 'modes of perception',

which could be called 'immediacy perception' and 'meaning perception'. When you are very tired and depressed, your meaning perception becomes blurred. But this is an illusion, caused by tiredness. On the other hand, when you are drunk and feeling jolly, the world seems to be all meaning. Then it is your immediacy perception that becomes blurred; you cannot even get your key into the keyhole.

On the other hand, there are times – perhaps when you are feeling happy and excited on a spring morning – when the two modes of perception seem to blend together perfectly. You have a wonderful sense of meaning, yet your 'immediacy perception' is fully operational.

What happens then could be compared to the film *The Dam Busters*, in which the British planes had to drop bombs shaped like billiard balls that bounced along the Moener Lake and hit the dam at water level. The problem for the pilot was to know when he was at exactly the right height to drop them. The solution was to place two spotlights on the plane, one in the nose, one in the tail, whose two beams converged at exactly the right height. So when there was just one spot on the surface of the lake, he released the bombs.

According to Whitehead, our most brilliant moments of insight happen when the two beams – immediacy perception and meaning perception – converge.

This, then, is Whitehead's 'refutation of Hume', and it is a break-through in western philosophy because it provides new foundations. The question 'Do we have free will or are we robots?' becomes absurd. Instead, philosophy can get back to its proper business, which Bertrand Russell defined as 'understanding the universe'.

And what of that other question: of the 'me' behind the scenes, whose existence was recognized by Fichte?

This was the problem to which Edmund Husserl devoted his life. It has always seemed to me that Husserl is the greatest of modern thinkers.

When he was at university, in the 1880s, philosophy was still struggling to throw off the toils of Bishop Berkeley, and the notion that 'meaning' is something created by the mind. John Stuart Mill, for example, argued that the feeling of logical certainty is no more than that – a feeling – and that all logic can be therefore reduced to psychology. This notion is called 'psychologism', and in its broadest sense it holds that philosophy, logic – even mathematics – can be explained in terms of psychology. This outraged Husserl, for it implied that all truth is 'relative', and Husserl could see that philosophy is never going to escape from muddle and confusion while it accepted such vagaries. So his starting point was the acceptance that logic deals with objective truth, not with relative ideas.

His first major work, *Logical Investigations*, was a sustained attack on psychologism, and an attempt to show that philosophy should be nothing less than a science.

This, of course, is what Descartes wanted to do when he asked the question: 'Of what can we be certain?' Husserl gave Descartes full credit for this, and even entitled one of his most important series of lectures 'Cartesian Meditations'. But, as we have seen, Descartes' problem was that he began with the wrong question: 'What can I know?', and failed to ask who was this 'I' who wanted to know.

Let me try putting this another way. In her book about 'female outsiders', *Alone, Alone*, Rosemary Dinnage discusses Bertrand Russell's affair with Lady Ottoline Morrell, and says:

> It is important to understand … that it was his
> underlying need to know whether anything could be
> established as true that shaped his whole mind …
> He himself felt that his search had made him into a
> 'logic machine', a 'spectator and not an actor', with a
> 'mind like a search light, very bright in one direction
> but dark everywhere else'.

What Russell had recognized was what Fichte had said a century earlier: that real philosophy demands an active attitude, rather than the passive one of the philosopher sitting in his armchair. To 'know' something merely with the mind is hardly to know it at all. Our whole being is somehow involved in true knowing. And when this happens, knowledge has a 'weight' that is not found in merely intellectual knowing.

Husserl's basic recognition is that *perception is intentional*; that when we 'see' something we fire our attention at it like an arrow. But if there is an 'intentional arrow', there must also be an archer who shoots it. In that case, Hume must have been wrong; there must be a 'real me' behind perception. And in trying to understand the way this 'real me' (transcendental ego) influences my perceptions and creates my life-world, Husserl saw himself as trying to 'unveil the secrets of the transcendental ego'.

This is also the essence of Husserl's revolution: that

consciousness is intentional, that it is active, not passive. It is like a hand reaching out and grabbing things, not just a searchlight. And Russell's own career is a sad example of what happens when a thinker stays in the 'Cartesian' mode too long. Russell spent his whole life asking: 'What can we know for certain?' And the result is oddly disappointing, for he never found a satisfactory answer.

But if, like Rosemary Dinnage, we remove our attention from Russell the thinker to Russell the person, we become aware of the consequences of his 'passive' attitude to philosophy – i.e. he totally failed to bring his interior philosopher and human being into line. As his second wife Dora put it to Rosemary Dinnage: 'Bertie could behave rottenly.' Until he was a very elderly gentleman he continued to pursue women, and to behave like an adolescent. As a person, he remained deeply unsatisfying to all the women he got involved with, and was dumped innumerable times. (I imagine his lifelong desire to screw any attractive female, from 15 to 50, was due to a gloomy conviction in adolescence that a person so ugly and preoccupied with ideas would remain love-starved, and by the time he learned different, the neurosis was too deep to be unrooted.)

But how could a person like Russell have benefited from Husserl's phenomenology? In fact, we may as well open the question out and ask, how could anyone?

Let me start by quoting the French phenomenologist Paul Ricoeur. He is talking about the 'reduction' or *epoché*, that method of 'standing back' and viewing things from a distance – rather like standing back from a large picture in an art gallery.

By means of this reduction consciousness rids itself
of a naiveté which it has beforehand, and which
Husserl calls the natural attitude. This attitude
consists in spontaneously believing that the world
which is there is simply given. In correcting itself
about this naiveté, consciousness discovers that it is
in itself giving, sense-giving. The reduction does not
exclude the presence of the world; it takes nothing
back. It does not even suspend the primacy of
intuition in every cognition. After the reduction,
consciousness continues seeing, but without being
absorbed in this seeing, without being lost in it.
Rather, the very seeing itself is discovered as a doing
[opération], as a producing [oeuvre] – once Husserl
even says 'as a creating'. Husserl would be
understood – and the one who thus understands
him would be a phenomenologist – if the
intentionality which culminates in seeing were
recognised to be a creative vision.

Husserl. An Analysis of his Phenomenology, 1987

But how?, the reader wants to ask. What is the trick of transform-
ing ordinary perception into creative vision?

We can begin by noting that poets do it all the time, and so do
great painters like Van Gogh. Read Shelley's 'Ode to the West Wind',
and you can feel the 'phenomenological vision'. Or look at a great
painting by Van Gogh or Vlaminck or Soutine. When I was

working in a tax office in Rugby in my teens, I remember my boss saying with disgust that he thought Van Gogh simply distorted everything he painted. He was missing the point: that Van Gogh was saying, 'This is how I see things when I put on my creative spectacles.' Rupert Brooke said that on a spring morning he sometimes walked down a country road feeling almost sick with excitement.

Brooke realized that he could bring on this feeling by looking at things in a certain way. And what was really happening when he did this was that he had somehow become aware that he could see more, become aware of more, by looking at things as if they possessed hidden depths of meaning. For it is true. He was becoming conscious of the intentional element in perception, that his 'seeing' was in itself a creative act. We can suddenly begin to see what Ricoeur meant.

Here is another way of putting this point across. A normal young male feels spontaneous sexual excitement if he sees a girl taking off her clothes. He feels this is 'natural', like feeling hungry when you smell cooking. But supposing he is looking through an art book with reproductions of paintings, and he sees a picture of a model taking off her clothes. She is attractive, and he stares at the painting, and then – let us suppose – deliberately induces sexual excitement in himself. How does he do this? In that question lies the essence of phenomenology. You could say that he looks at the picture, and deliberately puts himself in the state of mind of a man about to climb into bed with her. He ceases to see the picture from 'the natural standpoint' ('this is just a picture') and endows it with a dimension of reality. And it can be seen that he is again 'putting on his creative spectacles'.

The mind can deliberately change the way it sees things. Brooke wrote a letter to a friend in 1910, in which he described how he could wander about a village wild with exhilaration:

> And it's not only beauty and beautiful things. In a flicker of sunlight on a blank wall, or a reach of muddy pavement, or smoke from an engine at night, there's a sudden significance and importance and inspiration that makes the breath stop with a gulp of certainty and happiness. It's not that the wall or the smoke seem important for anything or suddenly reveal any general statement, or are suddenly seen to be good or beautiful in themselves – only that for you they're perfect and unique. It's like being in love with a person … I suppose my occupation is being in love with the universe.

We can grasp what Ricoeur meant by 'the very seeing is discovered as a doing'. Brooke is so excited because he realizes he can make himself see things in a certain way, and respond to them – just as an adolescent is excited when he discovers that this body can produce a heady brew called sexual excitement. And this is the very essence of phenomenology: you might say that phenomenology is a prosaic way of developing the mystical faculty.

Husserl's theories galvanized philosophy. But unfortunately, his chief disciple, Heidegger, undid all his good work by placing the concept of 'Man' (*dasein*) at the centre of his philosophy, instead of the transcendental ego and its hidden secrets. Heidegger dragged philosophy back into the muddle and confusion of his predecessors. Sartre was much influenced by Husserl and Heidegger, but he began by declaring that there is no 'transcendental ego', no archer to fire the arrow of perception. 'Intentionality' is mechanical, like the tides being pulled by the moon. We live in a meaningless world, so although we are 'free', there is no 'way' that will lead us out of the morass. But, as I pointed out in *The Outsider*, it is as impossible to exercise freedom in a meaningless world as it is to jump while you are falling.

Sartre at least declared his belief in political commitment to revolution. His main successor, Michel Foucault, was bowled over by Beckett's *Waiting for Godot*, and decided that this would be his foundation – the view that life is so comically meaningless that all talk of 'commitment' is futile. According to Foucault, history is like the fashion industry; it changes periodically, but no one can say it progresses. Foucault used his immense erudition to demonstrate the way that one 'fashion' (he called them *epistemes*) replaces another in an endless meaningless progression which (unlike Hegel's notion of history) never gets anywhere. Another complication was that Foucault was a homosexual with powerful sado-masochistic leanings, so his works became a disguised polemic, arguing for a kind of Dionysian explosion of repressed impulses. He regarded the 'motor' of evolution as the Will to Power, but, like Schopenhauer, felt this was purposeless. So Foucault merely represents yet another swing of the pendulum in the opposite direction.

The same, I would suggest, is true of another influential modern philosopher whose despair was based upon guilt about his homosexuality: Ludwig Wittgenstein.

Born in Vienna in 1889, the youngest son of a wealthy iron-and-steel magnate, his original ambition was to become an engineer, like his father, which is why he went to England to study engineering at Manchester University. An increasing interest in the foundations of mathematics led him to Cambridge, where he studied under Bertrand Russell. But he was morbidly pessimistic by temperament and obsessed by the idea of suicide. (Three of his brothers killed themselves.) When he hastened to join the army at the outbreak of the First World War, it was (he admitted later) with the hope of being killed. Throughout the war he carried in his knapsack the manuscript of his first book, later to be called *Tractatus Logico-Philosophicus*.

This book, perhaps the most influential work in modern philosophy, sprang out of Wittgenstein's craving to establish some kind of basic philosophical certainty, like Descartes' 'I think, therefore I am'. He considered the result to be the definitive answer to all the problems of philosopy – not because he felt he had arrived at some ultimate truth about the meaning of life, but because he argued that philosophy has no business with such questions. Philosophy, he said, can only deal with what can be stated precisely in language. And language has certain sharply defined limitations. It is a picture of the real world just as the Mona Lisa is a portrait of a real person. And just as a piece of matter is made up of atoms, so our world is made up of 'atomic facts', which can be combined into more complex propositions. We might compare it to the pieces of a jigsaw puzzle with which we can build a picture. But that picture can only be of the real world that lies around us. There is no way of including God or universal meaning, as certain idealist philosophers would like to.

Wittgenstein is not denying the existence of ethical or religious truth, but he is saying that it cannot be expressed in language.

This refreshingly down-to-earth view became the foundation of the philosophy known as Logical Positivism, which simply ruled out all forms of idealism as literally meaningless, like speaking of a square circle. But in the 1930s, he began to see that this view was too simplistic. Language is not simply a *picture* of reality. It is true that words are tools, but tools can be of many different kinds – hammers, drills, pincers, corkscrews ... And someone who uses words to create a fairy story is using them in a completely different way to someone who is writing a computer repair manual. According to Wittgenstein, fairy stories and repair manuals are different language *games*, and philosophy is only one among many such games.

Although the method of Wittgenstein's 'Linguistic Analysis' is far more complex than that of Logical Positivism, the aims are virtually identical: to destabilize the foundations of much that has always been accepted as philosophy.

It should be clear that Wittgenstein's view of philosophy has little in common with the one being offered in this book. For Wittgenstein, the question asked by Kierkegaard: 'What am I doing in this world and what am I supposed to do now I am here?' would be quite meaningless, for there is no way we can go 'outside' the world in order to answer it. But there are thousands of human beings who feel that such questions cannot be dismissed as misunderstandings of language. To feel that they have meaning is to suggest a world of meanings and values which exists outside this reality that surrounds and entraps us.

It has been worth discussing Wittgenstein here because he epitomizes a certain view of reality that strikes me as demonstrably inadequate. Clearly a book like this one, which takes as its starting point William James's question of how human beings can learn to live at much higher levels of power, has little in common with a work that declares that all questions of philosophy can and should be expressed in 'common language'.

The real problem with such a view is that it sets out to impose limits on the world and its meaning. In that sense, Wittgenstein and Samuel Beckett are setting out from the same starting point – denial of any meaning that is beyond the narrow and commonplace. They are trapped in Heidegger's 'triviality of everydayness', and insist that this is part of the human condition, and that insofar as we want something more than that, we are suffering from delusions.

Jacques Derrida, Foucault's most influential successor, was another swing back towards Hume. Taking from the linguistic philosopher Ferdinand de Saussure the view that words have no innate 'meanings', but vary freely in different contexts, he applied this notion to philosophy, which he sees as a kind of spume on the surface of the sea of language. Derrida says there is no 'underlying reality' (he calls it 'presence') and of course, no 'real me' or self. So it is again back to Hume.

The truth is that there are only two pockets in the billiard table of philosophy: materialism and idealism, and no matter how 'original' a philosopher, he is bound to end in one or the other.

But the real problem here concerns philosophy itself. Philosophers have always aimed at some 'system' that explains everything. We have to grasp that this is a mirage because – as Kierkegaard said – it leaves me *and my free will* out of account.

In mathematics, Kurt Gödel caused a revolution by demonstrating something very similar. Until Gödel, mathematicians had tried to create mathematical systems (like geometry) that consist of a number of self-evident axioms, and a superstructure of 'truths' built on these. Gödel showed that this is impossible – that in any such system, there are always certain truths that cannot be proved *within* the system; they can only be proved within a larger system still, a meta-system. (For example, a classroom full of philosophy students could discuss the question: 'How important is love to human development?', but the students will have to leave the classroom and fall in love before they can really understand the question.) And within that meta-system there are again truths that cannot be proved – and so on ad infinitum.

So whenever you hear of some philosopher – like Hegel or Foucault (or Beckett, for that matter) – who claims to have created a system within which everything can be explained, you are entitled to shake your head and murmur, 'Gödel'.

This happens to be an appropriate ending to a chapter about the 'strange story of modern philosophy', which began with René Descartes and his attempt to place philosophy on a scientific basis by 'doubting everything', and which has ended by doubting practically everything out of existence.

Clearly, it is time we began to look for our own meta-system.

Chapter Thirteen

Achieving Power Consciousness

Since writing the outline of this book 12 years ago, I have taught myself the basic method of achieving 'power consciousness' – that is, how to go about summoning it at will. Let me explain.

The experience that gave me the key had taken place more than a decade earlier, in 1979; but it took me several years to grasp its implications.

On New Year's Day, 1979, I was trapped by snow in a remote Devon farmhouse near a village called Sheepwash, where I had gone to lecture to extra-mural students. After 24 hours we decided we had to make an effort to escape. The farmhouse was in a hollow, and the thick snow made car tyres spin helplessly as we tried to climb out. It so happened that my car was the only one that could get a purchase, so with half a dozen volunteers pushing, I was able to get on to the level road that crossed a mile of white fields. It took more than an hour with shovels to reach the farm entrance and the main road. Now the path was open for other cars. I returned to the farmhouse for lunch before setting out in the darkening afternoon.

The snow on the narrow country lane had been churned up by traffic, but was still treacherous. In places where it was still untouched, it was hard to see where the road ended and the ditch began. So I was forced to drive with total, obsessive attention.

Within about 20 minutes I noted an interesting phenomenon. Sheer concentration was causing a glow of warmth in my skull, and I found I could increase it or decrease it at will. As a result, I was not becoming tired, because when my attention flagged, another burst of concentration brought the glow back.

Finally back on the main Exeter road, where I was able to relax, I noticed that everything I looked at seemed curiously real and interesting. The two hours of concentrated attention had somehow 'fixed' my consciousness in a higher state of awareness. There was also an immense feeling of optimism, a conviction that most human problems are due to vagueness, slackness, inattention, and that they are all perfectly easy to overcome with determined effort. This state lasted throughout the rest of the drive home. Even now, merely thinking about the experience is enough to bring back the insight and renew the certainty.

What had happened, of course, was simply that the need to sustain my attention without inner leaks had caused me to build up pressure far beyond its normal level. In short, response to the sense of urgency had created 'power consciousness'.

As if I had found myself in a strange place, I examined the effects with interest. The first thing to note was that everything seemed more *interesting*, so I kept turning my head to notice some tree or cottage I was passing. My perception seemed clearer, as if I had put on a new and more powerful pair of spectacles.

Now there was a sense in which this experience was not unfamiliar. When I left school at the age of 16 I had been offered a job as a lab assistant at my old school, with the notion that I could take my Inter-BSc degree, and eventually my BSc. There was only one problem. In the months since I left school in July 1947, I had decided that I wanted to be a writer, and found I was no longer interested in science. I knew it was only a matter of time before the Christmas exams found me out, but in the meantime, being back at school was infinitely preferable to the factory job I had been doing a few weeks before. But I was there under false pretences, and felt guilty and bored.

The physics master, an unpleasant man called Davis, took a dislike to me, so a smouldering resentment was soon added to the boredom. Every day I set out for work with an increasing sense of unease.

One day I found my answer. It lay in a small book called the *Bhagavad Gita*, to which I had been led by a reference in a T S Eliot essay. Its basic assertion was that the individual soul, the Atman, is identical to the ultimate reality, God or Brahman. All I had to do was to sit on the floor of my bedroom every morning and meditate on this, while focusing my mind intently on the identity of Atman with Brahman. And, to my delight, it worked. After half an hour of focused attention, I left home early and walked to school, a mile or so away, feeling curiously buoyant and optimistic. This had the same effect as that drive from Sheepwash – of making everything interesting. Walking through the slum streets where my father had grown up, I would pause to look with fascination at a cracked windowsill or a battered front door. At work, if I felt bored, I would find a corner where I could sit with my mind focused on the identity of Atman and Brahman. And within moments I had a marvellous sense of being in control of my life. It seemed clear to me that so long as I remembered this basic insight, I had an infallible method of renewing my sense of direction and purpose.

Of course, as the years went past, that ability to conjure up the sense of certainly was diluted by the complexities of earning a living. Yet it never vanished entirely, and on the drive back from Sheepwash I again experienced that sense of clarity and excitement. Above all, I now knew that states of power consciousness were possible. I merely had to focus my mind and keep it focused.

That explains why, when I went to the first night of *Endgame*, I rejected it as an attempt to convince me that black is white. When Clov says that the world is going out, but he has never seen it lit up, I could say 'Well *I* have,' and dismiss Beckett as a man suffering from laziness and self-pity – both his own fault.

In the years that followed the Sheepwash experience I occasionally tried to re-create it, but never very determinedly, for I suspected that I needed to start off with that sense of urgency that came from the possibility of landing in the ditch. But I continued all the same, for example, when driving from my home to Truro to do the weekly shopping. It gradually became clear that half an hour of focused attention is quite enough to renew the insight. I quickly discovered that, with practice, a feeling of control would rise up in me, and a certain cheerfulness would begin to glow, the feeling that Nietzsche describes when he says 'What is happiness?

The feeling that power is growing, that resistance is overcome.'
(*Antichrist*, 2).

This, I note, is also something I am inclined to call 'the
holiday feeling', that rising sense of delight we experience when
going to some unfamiliar place, and feeling that the world is full
of 'newness', merely waiting to be discovered.

Now philosophically speaking, this is undeniably true. That
sense of newness that we experience when walking down a street
in a foreign city, or simply down an unexplored country lane, is an
objective reality. If I happen to be tired or preoccupied, I do not
take in much of the 'newness'. But it is still there, just like all the
activities in a street that are recorded by a CCTV camera, whether
they are played back or not. So when Beckett's Murphy says that
the sun shone on the 'nothing new', he is being factually
inaccurate.

Among philosophers, the one to express the life-view of
Murphy in what he believed to be logical terms was Schopenhauer,
who writes in Book iv of *The World as Will*:

> We saw that the inner being of unconscious nature
> is a constant striving without end and without rest.
> And this appears to us much more distinctly when
> we consider the nature of brutes and man. Willing
> and striving is its whole being, which may be very
> well compared to an unquenchable thirst. But the
> basis of all willing is need, deficiency, and thus pain.
> Consequently, the nature of brutes and man is
> subject to pain originally and through its very being.

If, on the other hand, it lacks objects of desire,
because it is at once deprived of them by a too easy
satisfaction, a terrible void and ennui comes over it,
i.e. its being and existence itself becomes an
unbearable burden to it. Thus its life swings like a
pendulum backwards and forwards between pain
and ennui.

If we apply to this the test that Kierkegaard applied to Hegel –
'How far is this true *for me*?' – we immediately become aware of
what is wrong with it – or rather, what was wrong with
Schopenhauer. If his own life swung like a pendulum between pain
and ennui, then he must have been as subject to boredom and
depression as Beckett was. And indeed, this is precisely what we
learn from biographical writings on him – for example, the
section on him in Ben-Ami Scharfstein's *The Philosophers* (1980),
or the biographical sections in the studies by Bryan Magee (1983)
or D W Hamlyn (1980). We learn that Schopenhauer was born in
1788 into a wealthy middle-class family in Danzig, in which the
father, a wealthy merchant, was a stern disciplinarian with a
short temper. His wife, 20 years his junior, was herself a writer and
an enthusiastic socialite, who was not much liked by her son who
came to share his father's overbearing temperament and bad
temper. As Schopenhauer senior aged, he became a neglected
invalid, believed he was going insane, and committed suicide by
drowning when his son was 17. Schopenhauer became deeply
depressed. But he seized the opportunity to abandon the office his
father had consigned him to, and from then on became his own

master, studying Greek, Latin and philosophy. For the rest of his life he never had to work. Although highly sexed – in his own opinion far too much so – he never married, and took mistresses instead. He became a friend of Goethe, but the friendship did not last, and he became known as a sour and conceited man with never a good word to say about other contemporary philosophers, of whom he specially loathed Hegel (largely out of jealousy).

We can see that, like Beckett, this was a man whose problem was insufficient 'weight on the needles' (see page 83).

He was a hypochondriac and a morbid depressive, full of paranoid fears – at one point he even became convinced he had been poisoned by some doctored snuff.

Yet this was the philosopher who believed that he had come closer than any predecessor to solving the basic problem of human existence. He declares:

> … my philosophy is the real solution of the riddle of
> the world. In this sense it can be called a *revelation*.
> As such it is inspired by the spirit of truth – in the
> fourth book [of *The World as Will and Idea*] there
> are even some paragraphs that one might consider
> inspired by the Holy Ghost.

Clearly, this is not a philosopher whose view of himself one can take too seriously. Even Nietzsche, who began as a fervent admirer, ends by dismissing him as a nihilist, the heir to the Christian tradition, and the 'greatest psychological counterfeit in all history'.

In fact, Schopenhauer's indictment of life can be summarized in two words: the robot. We want something badly; we get it; then the desire evaporates and leaves us feeling like a boat stranded by the outgoing tide. This proves, says Schopenhauer, that all our desires are based on illusion.

It does nothing of the sort. It merely proves that *the mechanical part of us* can get used to anything. But our deepest values – let us say, a mother's love for her baby – are not eroded by habit, and neither are most of our moral values. When Schopenhauer says that without strong desires, we become subject to fatigue and ennui, he may be speaking about his own constitution, but he certainly has no right to speak for everyone.

In fact, he is willing to acknowledge this when he speaks on the subject of genius, explaining that geniuses possess a kind of freedom from the restless demands of the will because the present 'does not fill their consciousness'. This gives them, he says, 'that restless, zealot nature, that constant search for new objects of contemplation …' which preserves them from the mechanicalness that makes slaves of the rest of us.

What Schopenhauer is talking about here is what H G Wells calls, in his *Experiment in Autobiography*, freedom from primary needs and everyday urgencies. Wells says:

> … with the dawn of human foresight and with the
> appearance of a great surplus of energy in life such
> as the last century or so has revealed, there has been
> a progressive emancipation of the attention from
> everyday urgencies. What was once the whole of life,
> has become to an increasing extent, merely the

background of life. People can ask now what would have been an extraordinary question five hundred years ago. They can say, 'Yes, you earn a living, you support a family, you love and hate, but – what do you do?'

And here we can begin to see what Schopenhauer has left out of account.

Conceptions of living, divorced more and more from immediacy, distinguish the modern civilized man from all former life. In art, in pure science, in literature, for instance, many people find a sustaining series of interests and incentives which have come at last to have a greater value for them than any primary needs and satisfactions. These primary needs are taken for granted. The everyday things of life become subordinate to these wider interests which have taken hold of them, and they continue to value everyday things, personal affections and material profit and loss, only in so far as they are ancillary to the newer ruling system of effort, and to evade or disregard them insofar as they are antagonistic or obstructive to that. And the desire to live as fully as possible within the ruling system of effort becomes increasingly conscious and defined.

The originative intellectual worker is not a

normal human being and does not lead nor desire
to lead a normal human life. He wants to lead a
supernormal life.

In other words, people like Wells – and I imagine a vast majority
of readers of such a book as this – are 'originative intellectual
workers', people who enjoy thinking, to whom Schopenhauer's
description of what it is like to be human, is entirely inapplicable.

Wells goes on to say:

> Mankind is realizing more and more surely that to
> escape from individual immediacies into the less
> personal activities now increasing in human society
> is not, like games, reverie, intoxication or suicide, a
> suspension or abandonment of the primary life; on
> the contrary it is the way to power over that primary
> life which, though subordinated, remains intact.
> Essentially it is an imposition upon the primary life
> of a participation in the greater life of the race as a
> whole. In studies and studios and laboratories,
> administrative bureaus and exploring expeditions, a
> new world is germinated and develops. It is not a
> repudiation of the old but a vast extension of it, in a
> racial synthesis into which individual aims will
> ultimately be absorbed. We originative intellectual
> workers are reconditioning human life …

And then, one of his most illuminating similes:

> We are like early amphibians, so to speak, struggling out of the waters that have hitherto covered our kind, into the air; seeking to breathe in a new fashion and emancipate ourselves from long accepted and long unquestioned necessities. At last it becomes for us a case of air or nothing. But the new land has not yet definitively emerged from the waters and we swim distressfully in an element we wish to abandon.
>
> I do not now in the least desire to live longer unless I can go on with what I consider to be my proper business.

I feel these are not only the most important words Wells ever wrote, but among the most important words written in the past century.

Now Wells begins his *Experiment in Autobiography*, a few pages before the passage quoted above, by confessing that he is beginning to feel increasingly unhappy about his everyday existence, and the number of time-wasting distractions that prevent him from working. And it is easy to grasp what has gone wrong. Because he was brought up in the Victorian age, Wells was always inclined to idealize women. For him, they were wonderful, mysterious creatures whose ankle-length skirts concealed a world of infinite allure. So as soon as he became famous, he took full advantage of his celebrity to persuade as many of them as possible to unveil the mysteries and permit him into the shrine. And since gratification usually failed to satiate the hunger, he was still plunging into new affairs in his fifties and sixties. Which explains why, when he began his autobiography at the age of 68, he had the feeling that he had lost direction in pursuit of the Eternal Feminine, whose latest incarnation, a man-eater named Odette Kuhn, had been giving him hell.

I would argue that Schopenhauer was right in this matter at least – that enslavement to the sex drive is a certain way of wrecking your life – and that the unhappiness Wells expresses at the beginning of his autobiography is one result of his endless affairs.

But if a man of genius like Wells can be dragged into unhappiness by his sex urge, does this not tend to support Schopenhauer's case?

It might, if enslavement to the robot was inevitable. But it is not, as the following story demonstrates.

In 1958, Irvin Rubenstein and Jay Boyd Best, two zoologists working at the Walter Reed Army Institute in Washington, were conducting experiments involving the learning capacity of a simple organism called the planarian worm. Planaria are incredibly simple creatures – no brain, no nervous system – so they make excellent subjects for experiments in the lab. The two zoologists were trying to study how they could learn without a brain. They put some planaria into a closed tube containing water – which planaria need to live. They then turned a tap which drained the water out of the tube. In a state of alarm, the planaria rushed along the tube looking for water. Soon they encountered a fork; one branch was lighted, and led to water; the other branch was unlighted, and didn't. Soon, 90 per cent of the planaria had learned the trick of choosing, and when the water was drained off, they rushed along the tube and chose the lighted alleyway, whether it was the right or left fork.

But now a strange thing happened. As Rubenstein and Best repeated the experiment over and over again (with the same worms), the planaria began choosing the *wrong* fork. That baffled them.

One of them suggested that perhaps they were bored with doing the same thing, and the wrong choice was the expression of the kind of irrational activity – like vandalism – that springs from boredom. The other asked how *could* they be bored when they had no brain or nervous system? But a few more experiments seemed to indicate that the boredom hypothesis appeared to be correct. As the experiments continued, the planaria would just *lie* there, refusing to move, as if saying: '*Oh God, not again!*' They preferred to die rather than go looking for water.

It seemed so absurd that Rubenstein and Best devised another experiment to test the boredom hypothesis. This time they took *two* tubes, and a new lot of planaria. In one tube, which had a rough inner-surface, the water was down the lighted alleyway. In the other, which was smooth, it was down the dark alleyway. This was a far more complex experiment, and only a small percentage of the planaria learned which alleyway to choose. *But that small percentage never regressed.* They could do the experiment a thousand times and not get bored. Because they had been forced to put twice as much effort into the initial learning process, they achieved a higher level of imprinting – i.e. of purpose – and maintained it forever.

The relevance of this experiment to Schopenhauer and Beckett should be obvious. If someone fails to put sufficient energy into the learning process, they become subject to boredom, and might even prefer to lie down and die rather than make an effort. I had in my teens observed how many major writers, artists and musicians have had difficult beginnings, while those who have perhaps as much talent but an easier start in life seem to find it harder to rise above the second rank. Dickens, Shaw, Wells, Beethoven, Brahms, are examples of the first, Beckett and Schopenhauer of the second. It is as if the effort of dragging their cart out of the mud increases the vital drive of the first kind.

No doubt the difference could be explored by an experimental psychologist in terms of some part of the brain that stores mental energy. Determination has the effect of charging our psychic batteries, and it would be interesting to know where, in terms of brain physiology, the storage capacity is located. In their book *The Self and Its Brain*, Karl Popper and John Eccles speak of a concept called 'readiness potential', which is an electrical activity in the brain that precedes muscular action. An athlete about to perform the long jump builds up a high degree of readiness potential. They speak of 'modules' of the cerebral cortex which are in liaison with the self-conscious mind, and say that 'this is an action across the interface between the mental world and the physical world.'

Now it is plain that on my drive from Sheepwash in the snow, I also built up a high degree of 'readiness potential', which explains why I drove home in a far higher state of mental energy than usual. I know I built up this energy through sheer desperation to avoid landing in the ditch.

I have tended to label the kind of effort required as the 'if only …' feeling. My most memorable example was something that took place in Cheltenham in 1965. What happened was this.

While I was in a bookshop, our four-year-old daughter Sally got bored, and walked off to join her mother who was outside the shop, looking in the boot of the car; Sally trotted past her, and vanished into the rush-hour crowds on the pavement. When, ten minutes later, we realized she was missing, we rushed off in opposite directions, searching frantically. It was Joy who found her eventually, about a quarter of an hour later. My relief was inexpressible. And as we drove away, I found that I was seeing everything as beautiful. I can remember thinking, 'Aren't buses beautiful objects,' and 'Isn't exhaust smoke a delightful smell.' Obviously, the crisis had built up a huge amount of 'readiness potential'.

There is an interesting sequel. Some time later, my literary agent came to see me at my home in Cornwall, and I took him out to see the scenery. In the course of our conversation – no doubt we were discussing peak experiences – I told him about this episode. As I described my frantic anxiety, it became totally real, as if it was happening here and now, and as I looked at a cliff above the beach, I was suddenly back in Cheltenham, experiencing a flood of relief. Inducing 'readiness potential' had also induced Faculty X.

Now readiness potential also involves a determination *not to forget what has caused it*. Hans Keller, director of BBC classical music, gave an interesting example in an autobiographical broadcast in the 1960s. Keller described being in Berlin during the rise of Hitler, when fellow Jews were disappearing into concentration camps. He remembers praying: 'Oh God, if only I can escape from Germany I swear I'll never be unhappy again.'

What he meant, clearly, was that if he could escape with his life, the relief would create a permanent sense of gratitude. Did it do so? No. Keller was known among BBC colleagues as a bad-tempered, paranoid little man. Yet the fact that he spoke of the experience in a broadcast three decades later makes it clear that it made a deep impact on his awareness.

In effect, he had been presented with a clue that he could have used to create future peak experiences. *He merely had to re-create his state of anxiety in 1930s Berlin to 'perspectivize' any future anxieties.* And then, like Maslow's students recalling past peak experiences, he would have been hurled into a condition of delight.

What the story of Rubenstein and Best's planaria teaches us is that a certain degree of determined effort has the power to impose itself on the subconscious mind so we can call upon it when we need it. Note that I say 'subconscious' rather than 'unconscious', for we are not speaking of profound depths of the psyche, but of fairly superficial levels of memory.

I came across an interesting example when I was lecturing in a mid-western girls college in the early 1960s. I was talking to a class about Maslow and the peak experience when a young male teaching assistant remarked, 'Yes, I can do that.'

'You can do what?' I asked.

'Give myself that feeling.' And he proceeded to explain.

As a child, it seemed, he was prone to fidget in church, to his mother's irritation. One day, she whispered to him, 'If you do that just once more, you won't get any supper.'

He knew she meant it.

A few minutes later, he began to itch. Knowing it would mean going without supper, he resisted the desire to scratch, and soon it became agonizing. Then, as it reached a pitch where it occupied his whole consciousness, the agony was replaced by the peak experience.

Ever since then, he explained, he could do it at will. And as he said this, he gave a little wriggle of pleasure, and said, 'There, I did it then!'

What had happened was clear. As the desire to scratch turned into a kind of pain, he reached a point where discomfort turned to pleasure. And because it had cost him such an effort of will and self-discipline, some inner-computer had 'stored' the trick, so he merely had to re-create the experience in imagination – describing it to the class – to make it happen again. It is like the redial button on a telephone that saves us the trouble of redialling each separate digit.

In an earlier chapter (page 85) I used Granville-Barker's term 'the secret life', meaning that glow of inner power which has been stored by the vital batteries. It is what awakens in a mother as she breastfeeds her baby, or in a man as a pretty girl allows him to kiss her. You could say that it is inside all of us, but in 'peakers' it lies close to the surface, while in depressives it takes a lot of pumping to make it accessible. As discussed in chapter one (page 18), these are the people of whom Auden wrote:

> Put the car away; when life fails
> What's the good of going to Wales?

What causes life-failure? We have already dealt with that: the robot. When I make an effort, it sends a spurt of energy into my vital batteries. And when I do something mechanically, there is no spurt of energy. The problem is that boredom has a feedback effect until, like Maslow's personnel manageress who stopped menstruating, we feel dead inside. And it is easy to fall into this negative circuit. It happened to Beckett when he was young, so even the success of *Godot* was unable to arouse any cheerfulness. Life-failure has a certain quicksand quality that can easily trap the unwary.

But that depends on whether you permit yourself the luxury of deliberately-chosen intellectual pessimism.

On this point Nietzsche makes one of his few logical errors. He says in *Twilight of the Idols* (page 36): 'However contagious pessimism is, it still does not increase the sickliness of an age, of a generation as a whole: it is an expression of this sickliness. One falls victim to it as one falls victim to cholera …' But cholera can become an epidemic if it is allowed to spread. If Nietzsche had seen the effects of 'post-modernism' on the literature and philosophy of the last quarter-century, he would have had to acknowledge his error. But even so, he also said, 'I have made my philosophy out of my will to health,' in effect recognizing that his early admiration for Schopenhauer was a mistake.

Nietzsche, incidentally, was the only great western thinker who recognized that the basic answer was conscious reinforcement of the will to health – that is, of 'the secret life'.

Life-failure, then, is to a large extent a self-created malady. This can be demonstrated by the case of a 20th-century writer for whom I have always had a high regard, Hector Hugh Munroe, who wrote under the pen name of Saki. Born in 1870, he was a homosexual who was deeply influenced by Oscar Wilde, and the satirical stories and sketches he wrote for the *Westminster Gazette* are often as brilliant as the work of Wilde. 'The cook was a good cook, as cooks go; and as cooks go, she went.' 'I know it was dawn because the birds were making a twittering noise, and the grass looked as if it had been left out all night.' His sharpest sarcasms were directed against the respectable and, as with Wilde, it is easy to feel irritated by his determination to be witty and scathing.

However, his 1912 novel *The Unbearable Bassington* demonstrates an interesting change of attitude. The central character, Comus Bassington, is a charming, witty and spoilt young man, obviously much as Munroe saw himself, and who, like Saki's two other autobiographical heroes, Reginald and Clovis, takes pleasure in being perverse and rebellious. And when his whole future depends upon charming a wealthy girl into marriage, his obvious spoiltness alienates a suitable candidate into choosing a man she finds far less attractive. His only alternative is to allow himself to be sent to some remote outpost of the British Empire, where his Wildean gospel of perverse frivolity is completely inappropriate, and he dies of malaria and boredom.

For years after I read the book, I remembered the scene of Comus sitting on a bare, brown hillside, staring at the slow-flowing brown river and the ant-like activity of the workmen, and feeling utterly empty inside.

What is perfectly clear is that his creator has outgrown the gospel of frivolity, and its underlying assumption that life is meaningless. Although there is an author's note that declares: 'This story has no moral. If it points out an evil at any rate it suggests no remedy,' this was little more than a gesture of defiance. It is difficult to imagine him writing any more volumes about Clovis or Reginald, with their underlying assumption that witty triviality is always preferable to dull seriousness. That assumption, while amusing and even fruitful for a time (as Reginald and Clovis stories bear witness) cannot be sustained as a life-philosophy, and leads finally to emotional bankruptcy. It was from this that Munroe was suffering when, in November 1916, he was killed by a sniper's bullet in a shellhole in France.

Granville-Barker's play *The Secret Life* is a strange and fascinating work. In *The Outsider* I quoted from George Sampson's *Concise Cambridge History of English Literature* as follows:

> [*The Secret Life*] is a puzzling, disturbing post-war
> play [that] shows us the intellectual world reduced
> to spiritual nihilism. There is no clear centre of
> dramatic interest. The characters just come and go,
> and what 'love interest' there is seems entirely
> gratuitous. The dialogue is sometimes normally
> dramatic, sometimes philosophically enigmatic, as if
> the speakers had no other purpose than to ask
> riddles to which there can be no answer. Perhaps in
> no other volume is there so complete a revelation of
> the spiritual bankruptcy produced by the war.

It was, in fact, Granville-Barker's last significant work. Like Saki, he had written himself to a complete standstill. Yet although the atmosphere of the play is weary and nihilistic, it is clear from the title that Granville-Barker recognizes that this is only a temporary phase, and that the solution lies deep inside everyone. As Auden says in 'The Maze':

> The answer that I cannot find
> Is known to my unconscious mind.
> I have no reason to despair
> Because I am already there.

The Secret Life belongs to the same group of works as *The Unbearable Bassington*, Céline's *Journey to the End of Night* (regarded by Beckett as the greatest novel ever written), and eventually, Beckett's own *Godot* and *Endgame*. The difference is that Granville-Barker sees an answer to the nihilism that poisoned and devitalized Saki, Céline and Beckett. And so, by this time, should we. It lies in the secret life.

'The secret life' is what William James was writing about in what I regard as perhaps his most important essay, 'On Vital Reserves'. He begins by remarking that everyone is familiar with the phenomenon of feeling more or less alive on different days. Some days we sparkle with energy, and on others we feel oddly worn out. Most of us would attribute this to biorhythms, but it is undoubtedly far more than that.

Most of us feel as if a sort of cloud weighed upon us, keeping us below our highest notch of clearness in discernment, sureness in reasoning, or firmness in deciding. Compared with what we ought to be, we are only half awake. Our fires are damped, our drafts are checked. We are making use of only a small part of our possible mental and physical resources. In some persons this sense of being cut off from their rightful resources is extreme, and we then get the formidable neurasthenic and psychasthenic conditions, with life grown into one tissue of impossibilities, that so many medical books describe.

Stating the thing broadly, the human individual thus lives usually far within his limits; he possesses powers of various sorts which he habitually fails to use. He energizes below his maximum, and he behaves below his optimum. In elementary faculty, in co-ordination, in power of inhibition and control, in every conceivable way, his life is contracted like the field of vision of an hysteric subject – but with less excuse, for the poor hysteric is diseased, while in the rest of us it is only an inveterate habit – the habit of inferiority to our full self – that is bad.

Admit so much, then, and admit also that the charge of being inferior to their full self is far truer of some men than of others; then the practical question ensues: to what do the better men owe their escape? and, in the fluctuations which all men feel in their own degree of energizing, to what are the improvements due, when they occur?

In general terms the answer is plain: Either some unusual stimulus fills them with emotional excitement, or some unusual idea of necessity induces them to make an extra effort of will. Excitements, ideas, and efforts, in a word, are what carry us over the dam.

In those 'hyperesthetic' conditions which chronic invalidism so often brings in its train, the dam has changed its normal place. The slightest functional exercise gives a distress which the patient yields to and stops. In such cases of 'habit-neurosis' a new range of power often comes in consequence of the 'bullying-treatment,' of efforts which the doctor obliges the patient, much against his will, to make. First comes the very extremity of distress, then follows unexpected relief. There seems no doubt that we are each and all of us to some extent victims of habit-neurosis.

This dazzling analysis reveals the answer we have been looking for. When I was driving from Sheepwash in the snow, I was subjecting myself to 'the bullying treatment', then followed, as James says, unexpected relief and a sense of freedom.

He goes on to cite many examples of extraordinary effort in

the face of hardships, one of the most striking being the case of Colonel Baird-Smith, who was in charge of Delhi during the Indian Mutiny of 1857. Scurvy had filled his mouth with sores which also covered his whole body, and a wound in the ankle had turned septic. Cholera caused constant diarrhoea, and meant that he could not eat, and had to live on brandy and opium. Yet these did not keep him permanently drunk or stoned, but only served as fuel to keep him going. His drive sprang from the fact that he knew that, if he allowed himself to collapse, it would mean the horrible deaths of hundreds of women and children. So he held out until they were relieved.

But, as James points out, hundreds of slum housewives perform tasks just as heroic as a matter of course, and cites a French girl named Jeanne Chaix, eldest of six children, whose mother was insane and father chronically ill. On her wages from a pasteboard factory, Jeanne successfully supported a family of eight. As it happened, her courage and determination were rewarded by a prize from a philanthropic foundation, but, as James points out, vast numbers of similar cases receive no reward.

Now reverse James's question, and ask: what is it that prevents most people from displaying such qualities? The answer leaps out at us: laziness, self-pity, lack of imagination. So if we ask a thorough-going pessimist the reasons for his depression about life, and he answers in the style of the tailor from *Endgame*: 'Look at the world, then look at my trousers,' we think of Jeanne Chaix or Colonel Baird-Smith, and know he is being guilty of triviality. In such a person, a habit of passivity has caused 'the secret life' to shrink until it scarcely exists.

The vital question is obviously: how can it be strengthened? Shaw touched on it in *Heartbreak House*, when Captain Shotover, the retired captain of a whaler, tells Ellie: 'You are looking for a rich husband. At your age I looked for hardship, danger, horror and death, that I might feel the life in me more intensely.' The bullying treatment. He has instinctively recognized the lesson of Rubenstein and Best's planaria – that if you wish to reinforce an insight so it can never fade, you must put twice as much energy into the learning process. And this is something I discovered accidentally when driving back from Sheepwash, when putting twice as much concentration into the driving made me aware that consciousness can be pushed beyond its normal mechanical level. For what we are talking about is the *possible levels* of consciousness.

Driving from Big Sur to San Francisco in 1987, I began thinking about how many levels of consciousness I could distinguish. I began with deep sleep, which I called 'Level 0'. So Level 1 is dream consciousness. In that case, Level 2 would be the most basic level of waking consciousness – mere awareness – the kind of consciousness a sleepy child experiences when too tired to take much interest in anything; in Level 2, consciousness is simply a mirror that reflects the external world. This is 'awareness', but not 'self-awareness'. According to Bucke, this is the 'animal' level.

Level 3 is what Sartre called 'nausea'. 'You' are clearly present, but the world around you is 'merely what it is'. You feel stuck, like a fly on fly-paper. Eliot describes this 'meaningless' state when (in 'Portrait of a Lady') he talks about 'not knowing what to feel, or if I understand'. This is Coleridge's 'dejection', and Greene's state before he played Russian roulette. Greyness and boredom.

Level 4 is 'ordinary' consciousness, of the kind we are experiencing at the moment – the kind we take for granted as 'normal' consciousness. It is no longer too heavy to move, but in its lower stages it can be hard work. This is what Christina Rossetti meant when she said: 'Does the road wind uphill all the way?/Right to the very end.'

But this is only the lower end of Level 4. As we struggle on, things usually begin to improve as we 'warm up'. We begin to get the feeling: 'We're winning.' An odd feeling of inner strength begins to arise, an increased determination. At its upper end, Level 4 is close to 'power consciousness'. We feel we can 'do'.

In this state, we often find ourselves carried into the peak experience, which I regard as a kind of spark that leaps the spark-gap between Level 4 and the next Level, 5.

I call Level 5 'spring morning consciousness'. It is that feeling you get on lovely mornings, or on holiday, when the whole world is self-evidently fascinating and delightful, as T E Lawrence felt on 'one of those clear dawns that wake up the senses with the sun, while the intellect, tired after the thinking of the night, was yet abed.'

In this state you *know* life is good, and can now see clearly that the gloom of Level 3 was a delusion. You also know that we must learn never to give way to it. Our main ally is a high degree of courage and determination.

Level 6 is what I call 'magic consciousness', using the word 'magic' in J B Priestley's sense of pure delight. It is what a child experiences on Christmas day, or what a pair of happy honeymooners experience as they look out over a lake from the hotel balcony, and feel that all this is a dream come true. It is like Level 5, but 'permanized'. It can last for days or weeks.

Level 7 is what I have called Faculty X, when the mind seems so energized – or deeply relaxed – that other times and other places are somehow as real as the present.

These I regard as the basic seven levels of consciousness. Level 8 is the mystical consciousness described by Ouspensky (page 58), which seems to contain a series of paradoxes, such as 'I am nothing and everything,' etc. I feel that Level 8 is not, at present, our affair. Our business lies with the first seven.

Looking at these, you note that halfway up Level 4, when you begin to feel 'We're winning' – is precisely halfway to Level 7. It is as if you had climbed a hill, and now everything is easy going – down through the peak experience, spring morning consciousness, magic consciousness, Faculty X.

The peak experience is a sudden recognition that this is a possibility. Below Level 4, you suspect that you are going to be defeated, that all your efforts will terminate in Van Gogh's 'Misery will never end'. Above Level 4, you know this is untrue.

Now if we return to the recognition that, in ordinary consciousness, we are 50 per cent robot and 50 per cent 'real you', we can see that raising ourselves to 51 per cent 'real you' and 49 per cent robot is the all-important watershed. This is what I learned to do in that drive in the snow.

But you can also see that what really matters is to know about the seven levels of consciousness, and precisely where we are situated at the present. At the present moment, man stands on that dividing edge between uphill and downhill – Level 4. Yet, as we have already seen, most healthy people spend much of their time in the *upper* part of this fourth level. Most of us have already passed Level 4. All we need now is to recognize it consciously, to grasp it. If you look at the sweep of human history, from *homo habilis* down to modern man, you can see that, in a very real sense, we entered a new phase of evolution around 1740, when large numbers of people learned to use the imagination.

What then happened was the first step towards what Wells meant when he said: 'the fish is a creature of the water, the bird a creature of the air, and man a creature of the mind.' What has been happening since 1740 is that we have gradually learned to become accustomed to this strange new medium of the mind – a medium that does not even exist for the lower animals. Our mastery of this medium is happening so fast that it might even be said that we are learning to 'fly' rather than merely walk.

I also like to use another simile. When I feel low and tired, it is as if my 'attention' is scattered, like billiard balls all over a billiard table. As soon as I 'pay attention', it is as if the billiard balls come together in the middle of the table. And if I become deeply interested in something, it is as if they press together so tightly that they begin climbing on top of one another, forming a second row. Then, when I relax my attention, they separate and fall apart.

In these states of concentration and excitement, I catch a glimpse of another level. I can see that if I could get into a sufficiently concentrated state, the billiard balls would climb on top of one another until they formed a pyramid. And this pyramid would *never* collapse. Because my sense of meaning would be so deep, my interest in everything so great, that I would have passed the point where 'regress' or collapse is possible. I would be sustained by sheer perception of meaning. And for the human race, this would be the decisive step to becoming something closer to gods.

Postscript

About five years ago, I came across an important new clue.

Someone recommended me to check out a psychiatrist called George Pransky. I did, and discovered that he was the author of a book called *The Renaissance of Psychology*. Although it was out of print, I managed to get hold of a copy by writing to the author, who lived in New York.

He had been a Freudian, but had become increasingly disillusioned. It seemed to him that trying to cure patients of neurosis on the assumption that their problems were due to repressed sexual problems was mostly ineffective. And it certainly failed to work on his own marital problems.

At this point, a friend rang Pransky from Vancouver Island, and told him that he had discovered an extraordinary teacher called Syd Banks. 'Two years prior,' says Pransky, 'Mr Banks experienced an epiphany that was of such magnitude that he was scarcely recognizable as the person he was before the experience. From a few seconds of revelation and the resultant two days of revelation from that experience, Syd Banks was transformed from a shy, insecure person to a person of uncommon well-being, vitality and wisdom ... Here was a man with a pre-grammar school education who previously had difficulty giving a toast at a party of friends who was now comfortable sharing his new-found knowledge with people with advanced degrees.'

What had happened was this. Walking with a friend, Syd Banks had remarked: 'I'm so unhappy,' and his friend had replied, 'You're not unhappy, Syd, you just think you are.' This was the revelation that transformed Syd Banks's life. It was the recognition that we create most of our unhappiness through our negative thoughts.

When George Pransky told me this story over the telephone, I told him a joke that makes the same point. A man is walking to his neighbour's house to borrow his lawnmower, something he has done many times recently. He imagines his friend saying, 'Why don't you get your own lawnmower?' and how he will reply, 'But you see, it's not worth my while yet because ...' and his friend will say, 'That's all very well but ...' - and so on. When he finally knocks on the door and his friend opens it, he shouts, 'Oh, keep your bloody lawnmower!' and walks away.

The phrase I find most significant in Pransky's account is 'and the resultant two days of revelation'. The insight had to unfold in his mind until he grasped its full significance. And that significance was the realization that we are all the time creating problems that do not exist.

The situation could be compared to a coalman who comes home covered in black dust, so that everything he touches is smudged with black – even the soap and scrubbing brush he uses in the shower. Until he has removed the layer of coal dust he will continue to make black smudges.

Of course, we recognize this every time we experience relief after anxiety. I experienced it in Cheltenham when we found Sally, and buses looked beautiful. In fact, we even experience it on a smaller scale when we have mislaid something, and then find it – I have felt it many a time after searching the house for a book. But we fail to allow the significance of the insight to unfold in the mind. What Banks realized when his friend said, 'You're not unhappy – you only think you are,' is that thought is so intimately intertwined with experience that it is hard to separate them. It is rather like looking at a spring morning through a dusty windowpane.

But, as Syd Banks discovered, you only have to allow this insight to unfold in the mind, rather like one of those paper flowers that unfold in water. Once this happens, peak experiences begin to happen all the time, as they did for Maslow's students. Pransky remarked that Banks was the happiest man he had ever met.

Index